The Ways
We Choose

The Ways We Choose

Lessons for Life from a POW's Experience

Dave Carey

To: Bill Bacharach
May God Bless Your Choices

Dave Carey
01/01

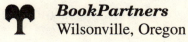
BookPartners
Wilsonville, Oregon

Library of Congress Cataloging-in-Publication Data

Carey, Dave, 1942-
    The ways we choose: lessons from a POW's experience / Dave
Carey.
      p. cm.
   ISBN 1-58151-042-X (pbk.: alk. paper)
   1. Self-help techniques. 2. Motivation (Psychology) 3. Carey,
Dave, 1942– 4. Vietnamese Conflict, 1961–1975--Personal
narratives, American.   I. Title.

BF632.C364 1999
158--dc21

                 99-047019

Cover design by Richard Ferguson
Text design by Sheryl Mehary

BookPartners, Inc.
P.O. Box 922
Wilsonville, Oregon 97070

To those POWs from Hanoi who have had innumerable influences on my life, and to my children, Jeff and Alyssa.

Contents

Foreword

For years I have read "Acknowledgments" in books and wondered how so many people could have been involved and helpful in getting a book from an idea to the finished product. I do not wonder any longer! There are so many people I would like to thank for their encouragement and help that the list would be very long. So let me just say that I am deeply appreciative to all those who have in so many ways encouraged and assisted me in this project.

In writing this book, I have worked from twenty-five-year-old memories, and total historical accuracy has not been my overarching goal. Rather, while trying to be reasonably accurate, I have told my story from my own vantage point — fallible memory and all. Some of the tricks our minds play on us over the years are undoubtedly in evidence.

My overriding intent in writing — indeed, the mission in my work and life — is that through all my efforts I may bring some amount of joy, hope, encouragement, and Christian witness to all with whom I have an opportunity to come in contact.

Introduction: Everyone Has a Story

I finished speaking. A huge Texan put his arm around my shoulders, saying, "Can I talk with you?" He gently guided me down a long hallway. "Dave," he began, "I understood every word you said today. The fact of the matter is, in this life, we are all going to get shot down, and some of us more than once." He then proceeded to tell me about the death, six months earlier, of his eighteen-year-old son. All the while, he was relating his story to the points I had just made in my talk.

Everyone who finds out that I was shot down and spent five and a half years as a prisoner of war in North Vietnam has an immediate reaction. They ask: "How did you do that? How could you do that for five and a half years?" As a professional speaker for the past thirteen years, I have been answering that question — to standing ovations.

I never started out to be a motivational speaker — or to write a book, for that matter — yet I'm always introduced as one. Now, if you want a little pressure in your life, try being introduced as a motivational speaker. You can just watch people folding their arms across their chests, as if to say, "Oh yeah? Well, just try and motivate me!"

Almost immediately, however, everyone gets hooked into what I say. Nobody dozes. They hang on my words and laugh; tears well up; they think intensely. And when I'm finished, they tell me what a great gift I have given them and how much they appreciate what I've said and shared. And the ones who were most skeptical are often the first to come and talk with me.

I am amazed at the reaction. How can a story from my life in the late 1960s and early 1970s have so much appeal to so many people — even to people who hadn't been born then? How can they become so intently focused on what I'm saying and, it seems, take so much away from it?

I think the answer is that the story I tell is, in essence, a basic human story. Extreme, yes, but nonetheless a fundamental human story: everyone, at least once, has had something very challenging, troubling, disturbing, and demanding happen in his or her life — something that has taken everything they had to get through it. We have all had our challenges, our uncertainties, our tragedies. Indeed, we all have our stories. The lessons I am able to draw have vast appeal and are directly translatable to everyone's story. Everyone has a story.

I have written my story for several reasons. One, quite frankly, is that audience members always ask if I have written a book. Most important, however, I hope — indeed, I pray — that this book will assist and reassure you as you live your story.

I mentioned that the question I am most frequently asked about my years as a POW is this: "How did you do that? How did you do that for five and a half years? How could you do that?" And that is the question that I want to try to answer in this book.

I don't believe it is good for us to dwell on the past unless there is something we can learn from it and apply in the present and the future. Therefore, there are numerous questions I am hoping that you, the reader, will reflect on as you read this book. Most important, I want to encourage you to read with this question foremost in your mind: "So what?"

"So what can I learn? What is of value in this for me?"

"What can I learn that would be useful to me in my life?"

"How am I going to get myself into the future?"

"How am I going to deal with all the change that is coming?"

"How do I choose to live my life?"

"How do I choose to do my job?"

"How do I live my life, do my job, day in and day out?"

"How am I going to deal with adversity? With tragedy?"

"So what?"

In short, I'm hoping you will do some real-time integration. Consider this story as an analogy for living life, for getting oneself into an uncertain future, for doing one's job, for meeting challenges, for dealing with tragedy, and for effectively handling life crises.

An analogy is merely a comparison. I am going to tell you a story. The inference is that a great many connections can be made between this story and your work and your lives. I can make some connections — some appear in the second part of the book — but I've learned that you can make far more connections than I can.

May God bless you,
Dave Carey

Part I

1

Shot Down

On rare occasions, something happens in life that is so significant, so forceful, so emotionally charged, that it is indelibly imprinted on the brain. The impression created by such an event is so strong that whenever it comes to mind, it is as real as though it had just happened moments ago.

One of those events happened to me on August 31, 1967. That day is as permanent in my mind as if it were etched on crystal. I can examine every detail of it. I can run it forward, backward, fast-motion, slow-motion, stop-action. On August 31, 1967, I was a twenty-five-year-old naval aviator, flying an A-4E Skyhawk aircraft from the flight deck of a US Navy aircraft carrier, the USS *Oriskany*. The *Oriskany* was cruising in the Gulf of Tonkin, about sixty miles from the coast of North Vietnam.

August 31, 1967, in the Gulf of Tonkin was one of those dull, gray, hazy days at sea: a day when the sky and the ocean are the same listless color; a day when there is no horizon, and everything from overhead to underfoot is the same dull gray. The carefully choreographed dance that is

Navy carrier aviation began about seven o'clock in the morning. Aircraft were given their preflight checks. Engines started. Post-start checks were completed. One by one, we taxied over the shuttle and onto the catapults that methodically hurled eighteen aircraft into the gray nothingness of the morning sky. Once airborne, we joined in formation over the ship and turned the noses of our aircraft toward the coast of North Vietnam.

In the summer of 1967, we were flying Alpha strikes three times a day. An Alpha strike was a concentrated effort by the air wing on board the carrier against a single assigned target. The carrier would launch a combination of fighters, radar control aircraft, air-to-air refueling tankers, and air-to-ground bombers. All the bombers would go after the assigned target. This cycle of Alpha strikes would be repeated several times a day.

That summer the opposition from the North Vietnamese was very stiff. They were receiving enormous supplies of anti-aircraft guns, ammunition, and missiles from the Soviet Union. As a result, the skies over North Vietnam in the vicinity of Hanoi and Haiphong were the most heavily defended of any conflict up to that time.

Very often, numerous surface-to-air (SAM) missiles were launched at the formation of aircraft. On one previous Alpha strike we had counted twenty-three SAM missiles in the air at one time. Our basic tactic was to make random turns ("jink") our aircraft about 30 to 45 degrees to either side of the path we intended to follow to the assigned target. Serious, extreme evasive maneuvering was reserved until it became obvious that a particular aircraft was being targeted and tracked. Had we committed to extreme evasive maneuvering whenever anti-aircraft fire was merely close to us, we would never have reached a target. There was so much anti-aircraft fire that we would have spent all our time evading.

The target on August 31 was a small railroad bridge six miles inland from the major North Vietnamese port city of Haiphong. As soon as we crossed the beach, the North Vietnamese started shooting. They always started shooting. That summer the sky above North Vietnam usually resembled what you can see in old World War II movies about air battles over Europe. All around us were black puffs of flak, detonations from anti-aircraft shells, and missiles racing through the sky riding tails of flame.

I remember it very clearly: that day, along with all the anti-aircraft fire, the Vietnamese launched two surface-to-air missiles in succession from way out in front of us. Back in 1967, the surface-to-air missiles were Soviet-made SA2s, the size of small telephone poles. The rocket motor kicked up so much flame and dust just getting a missile off the launch rails that on a clear day, from our cockpits high in the sky, we could see a missile launch from many miles away. And once the missile was in the air, the plume of flame from the booster rocket burned so brightly that we could watch it as it went across the sky.

I sat in my cockpit that day and watched the first missile. It just sat there, a little pinpoint of light on my windshield — a pinpoint of light that grew bigger and brighter, and bigger and brighter. At last it started to move on the windshield. I knew as soon as it started to move that it wouldn't hit me. (It's a relative motion problem: a collision course is one of constant relative bearing and decreasing range; thus, once the bearing starts to change — that is, when it starts to move on the windshield — it is no longer on collision course. For example, when a car is jockeying for position to get on the freeway, as long as there is some relative movement between it and the cars already in the lane, they won't hit each other…theoretically.)

So when the first missile started to move on my windshield, I immediately turned my attention to the second missile. It just sat there, another pinpoint of light on the windshield, getting constantly brighter and bigger. Finally I decided that if it was not going to move, I would have to.

My choices were turn as hard as I could either to my right or to my left, while simultaneously pulling the nose of the aircraft either up or down. Scattered somewhere to my left were sixteen other aircraft through which I would have to dodge if I turned in that direction. On my right was one aircraft.

I decided to pull the nose of my airplane up, then roll it to the right onto its back, crossing upside-down over that one airplane on my right, continuing the roll, and coming down on his far side, so I could continue on to the target. In aviation parlance, I was going to do a barrel roll around the airplane on my right.

It seemed like a brilliant idea at the time — until I was upside-down over that aircraft. The missile went right between us. There was a huge explosion. The fireball blew the tail section off my airplane, though I didn't know that at the time. My airplane stayed on its back. My forward motion stopped as though I had hit a brick wall. The aircraft started shaking, gyrating, and spinning through the sky. Nothing would focus. I tried to look at the instrument panel so I could figure out what was happening. It was just a blur.

The control stick felt as though it was not connected to anything. Both rudder pedals were up against the firewall. My airplane was tumbling through the air, no longer a machine capable of flight. It was spinning inverted, shuddering and bucking like a rodeo bronco.

Time seemed to slow down. Even though the aircraft was falling like a rock, the seconds seemed to pass like minutes. I fought to get control over my crippled machine. Every time the spinning nose of the airplane spun to face toward the ocean — the ocean that meant safety — it seemed to hesitate, and I'd think, "It's going to fly!" I'd move the control stick all around and kick the rudder pedals, trying to get my crippled aircraft to respond. It didn't. The nose would whip around, and the wild, gyrating spin continued.

It didn't dawn on me for long moments that I might not be able to fly this one. It stayed upside-down. I finally got a glimpse of my altimeter as I was descending through 4,000 feet. The realization flashed through my mind that 4,000 feet was not enough to do anything in a tactical jet aircraft — and certainly not enough to recover from an inverted spin.

Because the plane was upside-down, I had been literally hanging in my shoulder harness, upside-down with my head pressed against the canopy. My buttocks were several inches away from the seat cushion of the ejection seat.

The immediate problem was that an ejection seat builds up many times the force of gravity in its first couple inches of travel. The pilot is in fact sitting on top of a rocket, or mortar shell. The system is designed for the pilot's butt to be firmly against the seat bottom when the ejection sequence is initiated. Otherwise, the seat is accelerating so rapidly that when it makes contact with his butt, it has the force of a sledgehammer. Severe back injuries are the well-documented result of not sitting solidly in the seat upon ejection.

In an effort to get my butt against the seat cushion, I grabbed the control stick with both hands and, with all my strength, pulled my body up toward the seat. As my butt touched the seat, I let go of the stick with one hand and grabbed the ejection seat firing handle, located between my legs along the front edge of the seat. It was my singular good fortune that as the ejection seat fired, I had firmly pulled myself up against the seat. The canopy left the aircraft. I felt a blast of air as I ejected. Fractions of a second later, my parachute blossomed.

My time in the parachute was very short. I came out of the aircraft somewhere around 2,000 feet above the ground. Hanging beneath the canopy, I could hear the noise of rifles, pistols, machine guns, and anti-aircraft guns, and the scream of jet engines. The calm serenity of floating with a parachute was eerie amidst the sounds of war. When I looked down, the ground was rising rapidly to meet me. I landed with a thud in the center of a small village, coming down right between two thatched huts, with my parachute draped across their roofs.

It was very strange. There was no one around. The Vietnamese were all in their foxholes, or wherever they went for air raids. I quickly unbuckled my parachute and my helmet. I ducked out behind the huts and started running across a rice paddy. The mud was up to about mid-calf, so "running" was probably not the correct word. I had no idea where I was going, but I was going for all I was worth!

As I slogged my way across the rice paddy I could look up and see the rest of the airplanes flying away. When I was about halfway across, I saw that one of the planes was turning around and was going to come back toward me. I stopped right there and dug frantically through the gear in my survival vest, searching for the small two-way radio that we all carried.

I had held this radio in my hands a lot. The Navy insisted that we get them out every couple of weeks to check the batteries. Occasionally we played with them on the ship. I was very familiar with this radio.

But now, standing in the middle of that rice paddy, sinking in mud, watching that airplane coming straight toward me, I could not get that radio turned on. It was as though I had all thumbs on both hands. This radio was not complicated: it only had two switches on it, but I could not get those switches in the right places. In a near panic, my eyes riveted on that plane, I desperately tried to make the radio work.

It was by blind luck, or rather God's mercy, that just about the time the airplane boomed over my head, I somehow managed to press the right combination of buttons, and that little radio sparked to life. I intended to speak in my very best airline pilot drawl, cool, calm and collected. However, when I opened my mouth my voice was several octaves higher than normal, and I just started babbling, "It's me! It's me! Get me help! Get me out of here!"

I remember thinking to myself, "This doesn't sound very good." (In flight training, fledgling pilots are taught that it is preferable to die rather than sound bad on the radio.) The only good thing was that because I was babbling so hard, I ran completely out of breath and I had to pause to inhale. At that point I let my thumb off one of the radio's buttons, which allowed Dean, who was flying overhead, to get a word in edgewise. He said, "You know we can't come and get you." I couldn't think of a clever answer. Dean added, "I'll see you when this is over." And he flew away.

I stood out there in the middle of that rice paddy. I felt as though I were the only person in the entire world, out there, by myself, all alone.

Well I wasn't alone for very long. In the next instant I was surrounded by about one million North Vietnamese. That may be an exaggeration — but I'm sure there were at least nine hundred eighty thousand of them. I don't know where they all came from. They just appeared.

When I dared to look back at the little village, I was startled to see how many villagers were lining the far edge of the rice paddy. In the crowd that was materializing, I could see one old fellow who was about four feet tall. He had a rifle that looked six feet long. He began lowering the barrel in my direction. I immediately dove into the mud and did my best imitation of a rock. He started shooting. I could hear the rounds ripping through the air above me and I was certain that I was a dead man. In retrospect, I don't think he was really trying to hit me. I think he was just keeping me pinned down in the mud while they all decided what to do next. His plan worked very well — I didn't move. Soon they surged out across the rice paddy, capturing me in seconds.

They dragged me out of the rice paddy onto a dirt road and tied me up. They used miles and miles of rope to tie me up. You wouldn't believe how they tied me up. Rope was everywhere. Then, after they had me all tied up, they decided they wanted to undress me. They didn't untie me. Instead, one of the men reached between the ropes, grabbed handfuls of my flight suit and torso harness, and began hacking away my gear with a crude machete.

I had on all my flight gear: flight suit, torso harness, "G" suit, survival vest. If you've seen the movie *Top Gun,* you may remember Tom Cruise and "Goose" walking across the aircraft parking ramp, carrying their helmets. They have on flight suits, G-suits, and torso harnesses. That's exactly the way I looked. (Of course, I was a little better-looking than Tom Cruise, but that was a few years ago.) Anyway, the Vietnamese chopped away with his machete until all that was left was me, my undershorts, and my miles and miles of rope.

Simultaneously, some men in the crowd were obviously taking charge. They had on khaki shirts and were probably something like home militia or national guard. They formed a circle around me and pushed the rest of the Vietnamese back. Then they started knocking me around, beating, hitting, jabbing me with sticks, fists, and an occasional rifle butt. They and the crowd were yelling furiously.

The crowd became more and more excited, wanting to get into the act. They would all surge forward yelling, screaming, and trying to hit me or strike me with sticks or their fists. As the crowd closed in, the militia men would stop knocking me around and push people back away from me. After the crowd was pushed back, the militia again turned their attention to me. When the militia resumed beating me, the crowd would once again get excited and begin closing in on us. This cycle went on several times until the crowd was in such a frenzy that the militia men were beating their own people with the butts of their rifles to get them back away from me. Once again, I was sure I was a dead man.

The situation was on the brink of getting completely out of control. Fortunately for me, at that point the militia realized it. They beat the crowd back away from me one more time, quickly threw me into the back of a truck, and took me into the city of Haiphong. I was placed in a cell in an old prison. The cell had a very high ceiling, with little rectangular ventilation openings along the top of the wall. It was about eight feet by four feet. A wooden shelf, the bed, ran along five feet of the side wall.

Once untied, I retreated to the far end of the cell. Two armed guards were posted by the door, which remained open. All day long, peasants walked past the door of the cell, spitting, throwing rocks, waving their fists, and cursing. (I didn't speak Vietnamese, but I knew they were cursing!) I cowered at the far end of the cell and watched the parade of people. Slowly the shock wore off. I was having a hard time believing this was real. Surely this couldn't happen to me; surely I'd wake up soon.

Around dusk, I was taken out of the cell into a courtyard. My wrists were tied behind me and I was positioned behind a huge, rusting, double iron gate. The walls on either side of the iron gate extended only about ten feet in either direction. Beyond that the walls crumbled and broke down so that by twenty feet from either end of the gate there was no wall at all. About eight guards in full combat gear with bayonets fixed to their rifles lined up with me: two ahead of me, two beside me, and four behind me.

On the other side of the gate I could hear what sounded like a huge crowd. A voice on a bullhorn was whipping up the crowd. Finally, when the crowd was sufficiently excited, the gates were opened and the soldiers marched me through. The crowd roared. There were many cameras, both still and video, recording the scene as the soldiers triumphantly marched the American prisoner through the gate. I wanted to hold my head up rather than look beaten and dejected. I also wanted to be able to see what was happening. But every time I tried to look up, the soldiers would hit the back of my head with a rifle barrel, forcing me to keep my head bowed to show all the world how contrite I was. The filming went on for about ten minutes. As far as I know, those pictures and films never appeared in the media.

From there I was taken directly to a small room for interrogation. The room had a single bare light bulb hanging on a wire from the ceiling. A small table was set up at one side of the room; behind the table sat two men. One, dressed in civilian clothes, spoke very poor English. He told me he was the political commissar for the area. The other man was in uniform, and I was told that he was the military commander of the area. He spoke no English. The two of them began asking questions. They wanted to know what ship I was from, what type of aircraft I was flying, and what the target was. I told them only my name, rank, serial number, and date of birth — all I was required to tell them under the Geneva Conventions on the treatment of prisoners of war. (This was also all they were supposed to ask, according to those conventions.)

Every question was introduced by, and then frequently punctuated with, a lengthy political diatribe. The essence of it was something like, "Black American air pirate, capitalist warmonger, puppet of Wall Street, killer of women, children and old folk you are a war criminal and whether you live or die is now up to the People's Republic of North Vietnam. You have engaged in the atrocious murder of the Vietnamese people…." For a while I thought they were going to be content with repeatedly asking me the same questions and giving me their lecture.

Not so. Eventually the interrogator signaled the guards. They knocked me to the floor and tied a rope around one of my arms just above the elbow. They rolled me onto my side, ran the rope across my back and around my other arm. Using the rope for leverage and jumping up and down on my arms, they forced my elbows to touch behind my back. Then they tied the rope. The pain was astonishing: try touching your elbows together behind your back. I was certain my shoulders were coming apart. Numerous kicks and blows reinforced the agony. Then they stood me up and tied my wrists together, as closely as they could force them, in front of me. It was as though they were trying to cut my body in half with my forearms.

With additional repetitions of the lecture, I was told to think about my situation and my answers to their questions. Guards took me back to my cell. My arms slowly went numb from the pain. I retreated to the far end of the cell, and the parade of peasants resumed.

After what seemed like forever, but was probably at most two hours, the guards took me back to the interrogation room. Now the two men had an assortment of maps spread over the table, along with a ringed binder of plastic pockets holding five-by-seven-inch cards and a knee-board. (A knee-board is a flat, molded, metal clipboard that pilots of tactical aircraft strap around their thigh. It gives them a place to write and to carry frequency cards, weapons setting cards, maps, etc.). I immediately recognized all these as having come from my aircraft. My name was all over them.

The same questions started up again: ship, aircraft, target? The same political sermon accompanied them. I sat there looking at my maps, aircraft checklists, weapons setting, navigation, and frequency cards. I continued to answer with only my name, rank, serial number, and date of birth.

Finally the interrogator picked up the frequency card from the *Oriskany*. He said, "You flew from aircraft carrier *Oriskany*." In light of the evidence, I allowed as how that was correct. He then pointed to several A-4 checklists on the table and said, "You flew A-4 aircraft." Again, I assented.

He spread my map out on the table so that I could see a triangle around the railroad bridge west of Haiphong. I had drawn that triangle to highlight what had been our target just ten hours earlier. He put his finger on the triangle and said, "This bridge was target." I agreed with him.

The interrogator launched into a wordy lecture on the illegality and immorality of the war in Vietnam. He repeated over and over, "You are a black American air pirate, war criminal, capitalist warmonger, puppet of Wall Street, killer of women, children and old folk. We will kill you, you will never return to your home." He repeatedly praised the cause and sacrifice of the Vietnamese people. This would be the first of innumerable repetitions of this lecture I would hear over the years.

At last he told the guards to untied me. My arms were completely numb and useless. They felt like they were on fire as the blood rushed back into them. I was then bound more loosely, blindfolded, and loaded into the back of a truck. There were numerous men, who I presumed were soldiers, sitting along the sides of the truck. I was shoved into a corner on the floor near the front of the truck bed. All night long we traveled. We bounced over bone-jarring potholes, stopped and started and waited. It took all night to get to Hanoi, a journey of about fifty miles.

I was exhausted. I may have dozed, but never for more than a few minutes. My mind was racing. Could I escape? My arms still weren't working; there were dozens of Vietnamese soldiers in the truck. How could this be happening to me? I was invincible — this kind of thing happened to other guys, not me. What was going to happen to me?

2

Welcome to Hanoi

Just before dawn we arrived in downtown Hanoi at a huge prison complex, which I would learn my American predecessors had previously named the "Hanoi Hilton." I was led to a cell, which I would later learn was the infamous "knobby room" in a section of the prison Americans had already named "New Guy Village." The walls of the cell had tennis-ball-sized lumps of concrete all over them, hence the name "knobby."

The guards shoved me into the cell, removed my blindfold and slammed and locked the door. The cell was about 12 feet square. Looking around in the dim light, I could see a table on the far side of the room, with a stool in front of it and a couple of chairs behind it. I was able to wiggle my arms out of the loosely tied ropes. In a state of complete exhaustion, I climbed onto the table and soon was fast asleep.

The sound of the door opening awakened me. A guard walked into the cell. I scrambled off the table and desperately tried to remember where I was. As I managed to get onto my feet, he approached the table. From out of nowhere he swung his fist and hit me on the jaw. I went sprawling onto the floor. The guard, who I would later find out was nicknamed "Lantern Jaw," proceeded to tell me that I was not ever, repeat not ever, to get on that table again. Although Lantern Jaw did not speak a word of English and I spoke no Vietnamese, there was no doubt in my mind what he was telling me.

Later that morning a meal was delivered to the cell. It consisted of a bowl of rice and a bowl of some kind of soup — a bowl of hot water with some greens in it. I would learn that this was termed "sewer green soup." It was disgusting, but I forced it down; I knew I had to keep my strength up.

Soon after that an interrogator arrived. He seated himself behind the table and instructed me to sit down on the stool. He began an almost verbatim repetition of the lectures I had received in Haiphong, though his were lengthier and better rehearsed. Eventually his questions started. Essentially, he wanted to know two things: What were the immediate future targets in and around Hanoi, and when would they be attacked? I responded with my name, rank, serial number, and date of birth. His lectures became more impassioned and more threatening.

After some time he motioned to the guards, who knocked me to the floor. They took a strap and tied my arms above the elbows, jumping up and down on me till my elbows again touched behind my back. Then they sat me up on the floor with my legs bent and crossed, "Indian fashion." The strap was run up over one shoulder, down around my ankles where they crossed, and back up over the other shoulder to where my elbows were tied together. With lots of attendant hitting, pushing, and pulling, my elbows were drawn up away from my back and my torso was bent down toward my ankles. The pain was indescribable.

Sometime during this process, I began screaming. For that I was gagged with a rag-wrapped stick which was put across my open mouth and tied to my head. I was almost choking to death. I quickly decided that yelling and screaming was not a good idea. When they finally had me trussed up into a ball on the floor, the interrogator told me that I would be left to think about my crimes. He left, and a guard sat behind the table, smoking cigarettes. He didn't speak English, but he had been instructed to say to me periodically, "You talk?"

I lay on the floor, knowing that my arms, shoulders, knees, hips and back were all being torn apart. The intense pain didn't seem to lessen with time. I don't know how long I lay there, perhaps an hour or two; finally, when the guard said, "You talk?" I nodded my head "Yes."

He came around the table and untied me. My body wasn't working very well, so he pulled me up onto the stool and went to get the interrogator. When the interrogator returned, he immediately launched into the lecture, adding how foolish I was to resist them. They could, and would, make me answer whatever questions they asked. Eventually he got back around to his questions. I breathed deeply and responded with my name, rank, serial number, and date of birth. He was furious and repeated the lecture, questioning, and threatening tirade. It did not last as long as the first time, and soon the guards were again trussing me up on the floor.

This process was repeated several times. Each time I was untied for a shorter period of time. Eventually they wised up and didn't untie me. Instead, the interrogator came in, pulled his chair up beside me, and lecture/questioned while I was still in a ball on the floor.

One of the ironies of the situation was that I did not know the information he wanted. Targeting information came to the ship via message traffic, once or twice every twenty-four hours. No one knew what the future targets were. At one time I tried to explain that to him. He wasn't buying the explanation.

Another time, I told him that I was just a stupid junior officer. I knew nothing. He only had to look at his own army to realize that junior officers were not entrusted with that kind of information. I told him that if he wanted to know these things, he needed to go find a commander and ask him. He wasn't buying that, either.

Unbelievably, the pain increased steadily. My arms, shoulders, back, and hips were all being torn and dislocated. I begged them to kill me. But they wouldn't kill me. They just hurt me.

Eventually I reached the point where I absolutely knew that if the pain kept up, I was going to go insane. I did not want to go crazy. Even as a junior officer I had my own small fund of military secrets. I knew that if I were crazy, I would have no control over what I might say. I decided I would hold out as long as I possibly could, until the last possible second, and try lying. The last possible second arrived all too soon.

I wish I could say that I held out for weeks. I didn't. It took about a day and a half — I lost track of time at that point. I had already tried some Rambo stuff. That only works in the movies. I got to the point where I knew I was going to go crazy, so I started to lie.

The interrogator asked "What are the targets in Hanoi?" I made one up: "The thermal power plant."

"Other targets?" he demanded. I made some others up. "You see," he cried, "you do know!"

And the lecture started. "Foolish American, you cannot resist our questions. We will kill you. You have disappeared. No one cares about you. You will never see your family again…."

"When will thermal power plant be attacked?" I told him I didn't know. He signaled the guards to tighten the ropes.

"Eight o'clock tomorrow morning," I said. He wanted more times for other targets. I made up some days and times.

I lied about everything. Interrogators write everything down, and they have memories like elephants. So I'm lying about everything, and he's writing it all down.

Finally they finished with me, untied me, and left. I do not know how to describe the pain. I could not get up off the floor. My arms didn't work anymore — they didn't work right for many weeks. I ate by wiggling on my stomach and sticking my face in a bowl of rice or soup.

But worse than the pain in my body was that in my mind. I could not focus my thoughts. Everything was confused. It is the only time I have ever been like that in my life. I could not pick a subject and think about it. It was as though my mind was out of control. The subject I wanted to think about was all the lies I had told. I knew they would be back, and I wanted to be able to start with the same set of lies. But I could not force my mind to focus.

My mind, out of control, bounced around the inside of my head. Strange, unrelated thoughts flashed in and out: my home in Jeannette, Pennsylvania; the dog I had when I was a kid; the first car I bought. I was desperate to get my mind under control, and I could not.

Then into my head came the first line of the Twenty-third Psalm. It kept recurring: "The Lord is my shepherd." I didn't want to think about it, either. I wanted to think about the lies I had told, so that when they returned I could at least start with the same lies. Nonetheless, I discovered slowly that if I thought about that phrase, "The Lord is my shepherd," I could focus on it. So I returned to it constantly.

I had memorized the Twenty-third Psalm when I was a small child in Sunday school. Over the years, I had drifted away from church. I am ashamed to admit that at that point in my life, it had probably been at least twelve years since I had thought of the Twenty-third Psalm.

But now it was there, and if I thought about that line, "The Lord is my shepherd," I could concentrate. I worked on it for days, until from somewhere far back, I was able to dredge up the entire psalm. Once I had done that, I had control of my mind back. I don't think that was any accident.

By now perhaps three or four days had passed. I had my mind back and I could think, though my arms still didn't work. I still couldn't stand up. I was still eating by wiggling on my belly and sticking my face in a bowl of rice, but I could think.

Thinking turned out to be a mixed blessing. Depression was not something I had ever been familiar with, but for many days I felt lower than whale dung. The biggest issue was this: I had not been able to do what I had been trained to do.

I had been trained that in a situation like this, if I were tough enough, held out long enough, my captors would tire of me, give up in frustration, and put me in a compound with other prisoners. That's the way it had been in Korea, and my training came out of the Korean conflict. The military is always a war behind in some respects.

In addition to my training, I had seen every John Wayne movie ever made. I knew how an American fighting man conducted himself in situations like this. I had not lived up to that. I had "cracked," "broken." It didn't matter that all I had done was lie. I was trained to give only name, rank, serial number, and date of birth. I hadn't been able to resist.

How would I ever be able to face my squadron mates again? My Navy? My family? I was miserable. It took weeks to get over that depression, and it took many days to arrive at the realization that all that was possible in this situation was to do the best that I could. Either my best would be acceptable to the Navy and at home, or it wouldn't, but that was all I could do — my best. I was going to be able to say, "I did my best." And that was all.

I knew then, very early and very clearly, that I was not a superman. Nor was I nearly as tough as I would have liked to imagine myself. If they had tortured me and broken me once, they could do it again. The experience was very humbling.

I was miserable. I wouldn't learn for months that what I had gone through was standard treatment for incoming POWs. Almost to a man, that scenario was played out with each new captured American. In retrospect, I think the North Vietnamese wanted to establish clearly who was in charge and who was the captive. They must have known they were getting worthless information. For me, though, it was devastating.

I had one bit of good fortune: the North Vietnamese were so busy at that time, August and September of 1967, with Americans newly shot down and captured that they didn't have a lot of time or energy for me. I was a rather ignorant junior officer, after all.

A week had passed since I arrived in Hanoi, and it seemed like a year. I was able to get up off the floor, my hands and arms were still numb, I could think, and I was beginning to deal with the depression. Then the door opened and two North Vietnamese officer/interrogators walked in. They sat down behind the table, and the guards sat me down on the stool facing them across the table. I thought to myself, "Oh no, here we go again."

One officer spoke English, more or less. The other did not. The English-speaker began asking some rather benign questions, always laced with the standard lecture: war criminal, air pirate, puppet of Wall Street. He asked where my home was in the United States. Did I have a family? I answered with my name, rank, serial number, and date of birth. I figured I might as well start at the beginning. The ratio of lecture to questions increased.

As the English-speaker lectured me and asked an occasional question, the other officer was becoming noticeably more and more agitated. He began talking, then yelling at me in Vietnamese. Standing up, he began pacing around the room, all the while becoming louder and more agitated. His partner said a couple of things to him in Vietnamese; I thought it sounded like he might be trying to calm this fellow down.

I was relatively happy. As long as they were talking, or even yelling, I didn't need to say anything. At length, the one who was pacing and yelling walked up behind me and hit me so hard that he knocked me off of the stool. He then began kicking me and pounding me with his fists.

The English-speaker jumped up and came to my rescue. He pulled his partner off me, calmed him down, and led him out of the room. Shortly the English-speaker returned. He helped me up onto the stool, stuck a cigarette in my mouth, lit it and one for himself. He proceeded to tell me about his partner.

"American air pirates have killed my partner's entire family. His village was bombed killing his wife, children, parents, grandparents, aunts, uncles, everyone, none survived. He is not mentally a well man. He grieves so. His mind is clouded with hatred and revenge. You must be very careful how you act and what you say around him. He is not stable. You must be very respectful and sorry."

About then his partner came back into the room and reseated himself behind the table. The English-speaker started the lecturing/questioning. I stuck to name, rank, serial number, date of birth. In a matter of minutes his partner was back on his feet pacing, and mumbling to himself.

A few more minutes and the partner came completely unglued. Screaming and shouting, his face blood-red, he dove across the table at me. Knocking me to the floor, he began beating me with his fists. The English-speaker was on his feet and trying to calm him down. He swung at the English-speaker, knocking him away. He returned to beating and kicking me. The English-speaker called for help.

Through the door came four or five guards. For a few minutes it was a free-for-all. The partner was shouting and swinging at anyone who got close to him, all the while sitting on top of, and beating on, me. After lots of yelling and grabbing and many more blows, they finally subdued him. He was mumbling and sobbing as guards led him from the room.

The English-speaker returned, got me back up on the stool, stuck another cigarette in my mouth, lit it, and repeated his partner's history, again cautioning me about cooperation and respect.

Then the door burst open and his partner rushed in wielding a huge machete. He was sobbing and screaming and coming directly at me. As he began to swing the machete, I rolled off the stool onto the floor. The machete struck the tile floor in a shower of sparks as I rolled away from it. The next swing just missed me as I rolled under the table.

The English-speaker was on his feet, yelling for the guards, who burst in. The machete flashed again. I kept rolling across the floor. The guards circled him cautiously. He was swinging the machete wildly, mostly in my direction. At an opportune moment, the guards rushed him, wrestled him to the floor, and took the machete away.

They half-led, half-dragged him from the room, struggling all the way. The English-speaker followed. I lay on the floor panting, thankful that he had not connected with the machete. They never returned.

In hindsight, I know that this was a rather standard, if overly dramatic, interrogation ploy: "good guy/bad guy." These two had merely been practicing their routine. In fact, I had been exposed to a much milder version of the routine in my training before leaving the United States. Nonetheless, when it was happening in that knobby room in Hanoi, my life was flashing before my eyes. I was terrified. It was only much later that I realized it had been an act. As far as I was concerned, those guys could have won an Oscar. I was sure I was dead meat.

I was being fed twice a day. Each meal consisted of a bowl of soup, usually of unknown origins, and a bowl of rice. Several days later, yet another North Vietnamese officer came into the room. Along with the standard lecture, he gave me a mosquito net, a small pot for the boiled water that was delivered twice a day, a pair of black shorts, and a black T-shirt.

After a week and a half, I was taken out of the room and led to another building across a small courtyard. A rudimentary shower had been built there, with a rusty water pipe that had been run into the small room. It was a moldy, slimy pit. I stood there in my rags. The cold water running down over me felt so good!

On my return to the knobby room, I noticed another set of prison clothes hung over a line in the corner of the courtyard. It was the only hint I had seen that there might be someone else held here.

Later that day a new interrogator came into my room. He had a rolled up paper under his arm. It looked to be the size of a blueprint. He began to question me about the United States Navy. He asked me how many attack carriers the Navy had, I stuck to name, rank, serial number and date of birth. He really didn't care what I said and answered his own question. Which was good because I didn't know how many carriers the Navy had.

It became obvious that he was showing me how much he knew about the Navy. He asked me, "What are the hull numbers and radio call signs of those carriers?" (Another question I didn't know the answer to.) No matter, he proceeded to tell me the answers. Eventually his questions turned to the command and control structure of the forces operating in and around Vietnam. At that point he unrolled his scroll of paper.

On the paper was the complete wiring diagram for the United States military operating in South East Asia. At the top was the President of the United States. Then came the Secretary of Defense, the Secretaries of the various services, the Joint Chiefs of Staff… The wiring diagram had the chain of command and all of the operating units on it down to individual ships, squadrons, and ground forces. It was amazing in its detail.

Along the bottom edge was one blank space. He carefully explained to me that what he needed was the name for this blank space. It belonged to a group of US Navy PT boats that operated out of South Vietnam and made raids along the southern coast of North Vietnam. At briefings aboard the carrier, we were told when these PT boats would be operating and that they would give some sort of identifying signal, which changed each day, so we would know they were friendlies.

He carefully explained all this to me. I was amazed at how much he knew. Finally he popped the question he was interested in: "What is the radio call sign of these PT boats?" That was what was blank on his chart — and as far as I could see, the only blank.

I responded with name, rank, serial number, and date of birth. Now he began in earnest with the standard lecture and threats. I didn't answer. Eventually he called in the guards and they began knocking me around. Finally they threw me to the floor and brought in the straps. As they began strapping my arms, he asked again for the call sign of those boats.

I lay there on the floor, feeling my arms getting even more numb, knowing exactly where this was going. I couldn't remember the call sign. However, as I considered the condition I was already in, I didn't think it would be prudent for me to go through torture again if I could get out of it cheaply. I said, "The call sign is Dragonfly."

He motioned for the guards to let me up and untie me. He very carefully wrote "Dragonfly" in the empty space on his chart. All the while, he was lecturing me on the foolishness of resistance. They could force me to say and do whatever they chose. The sooner I quit being so obstinate, the better it would be for me. He left.

I was convinced this was all insanity. He was willing to torture me for a radio call sign for his stupid chart. Another guy was trying to kill me with a machete. Who knows what they might think of next? I didn't have to wonder very long. Within days, yet another officer entered my room. He introduced himself as the camp commander.

3

Roommates

The camp commander explained to me — along with the normal lecture, of course — that soon I would move, and because of their lenient and humane policy, I was to have a cellmate. That really got my attention. He then laboriously went over all of the camp regulations, explaining each in infinite detail. These camp rules were eventually smuggled out by a released prisoner:

February 1967
In accordance with the prevailing situation in the camp and following the recent educational program of the criminals about the policy toward them and based on:

1. The policy toward the American criminals already issued.

2. The provision of detaining the blackest criminals in the Democratic Republic of Viet Nam (DRVN).

3. The inspection and implementation [sic] of the camp regulations by the criminals in the past.

4. In order to insure the proper execution if the regulations, the camp commander has decided to issue the following new regulations which have been modified and augmented to reflect the new conditions. From now on the criminals must strictly follow and abide by the following provisions:

a. The criminals are under an obligation to give full and clear written or oral answers to all questions raised by the camp authorities. All attempts and tricks intended to evade answering further questions and acts directed to opposition by refusing to answer any questions will be considered as manifestations of obstinacy and antagonism which deserves strict punishment.

b. The criminals must absolutely abide by and seriously obey all orders and instructions from the Vietnamese officers and guards in the camp.

c. The criminals must demonstrate a cautious and polite attitude [toward] the officers and guards in the camp and must render greetings when met by them in a manner already determined by the camp authorities. When Vietnamese officers and guards come to the rooms for inspection or when they are required by the camp officer to come to the office room, the criminal must carefully and neatly put on their clothes, stand at attention, bow a greeting, and await further orders. They may sit down only when permission is granted.

d. The criminal must maintain silence in the detention rooms and not make any loud noises which can be heard outside. All schemes and attempts to gain information and achieve communication which [sic] the criminals living next door by intentionally talking loudly, tapping the walls, or other means will be strictly punished.

e. If any criminal desires to ask a question, he is allowed to say softly only the words "Boa cao." The guard will report this to the officer in charge.

f. The criminals are not allowed to bring into and keep in their rooms anything that has not been so approved by the camp authorities.

g. The criminals must keep their rooms clean and must take care of everything given to them by the camp authorities.

h. The criminals must go to bed and arise in accordance with the orders signaled by the gong.

i. During alerts the criminals must take shelter without delay. If no foxhole is available, they must go under their beds and lay close to the wall.

j. When a criminal gets sick, he must report it to the guard who will notify the medical personnel. The medical personnel will come to see the sick and give him medicine or send him to the hospital if necessary.

k. When allowed outside his room for any reason, each criminal is expected to walk only in the areas as limited by the guard in charge and seriously follow all his instructions.

l. Any obstinacy or opposition, violation of the preceding provisions, or any scheme or attempt to get out of the detention camp without permission are all punishable. On the other hand, any criminal who strictly obeys the camp regulations and shows his true submission and repentance by his practical acts will be allowed to enjoy the humane treatment he deserves.

m. Anyone so imbued with a sense of preventing violations and who reveals the identity of those who attempt to act in violation of the foregoing provisions will be properly rewarded. However, if and [sic] criminal is aware of any violation and deliberately tried to cover it up, he will be strictly punished when this is discovered.

n. In order to assure the proper execution of the regulations, all the criminals in any detention room must be held responsible for any and all violations of the regulations committed in their room.

Signed
The Camp Commander

While the officer droned on and on through the rules, I was still focused on his initial statement. My mind was churning — a roommate? I hadn't seen even a sign of another American since being shot down. A roommate!

Later that day a guard came in and indicated I should roll up all my stuff. I did that in an instant. He blindfolded me and led me through several parts of the prison. I ended up in a cell in a building I would later learn was called the "Golden Nugget," in a section of the prison we called "Las Vegas." All of the buildings had been named for casinos.

The cell was about six feet by twelve. Along each side wall was a two-foot-wide wooden bench; those were the beds. The door had a small peep door in the upper center part. To the left of the door was one barred window, boarded shut. Across the walkway in front of the cell, parallel to the building, was a line of wash areas. Each wash area was about eight feet square, separately enclosed with its own door, and either a concrete cistern or sink area which held water. I waited expectantly to see the first friendly face in two weeks.

About an hour later, the door opened and another American was shoved through it with his stuff. The camp commander reminded us of the rules. The door closed and locked.

We fell into each other's arms and began crying. It was such a relief to see, touch, and talk to another American. We introduced ourselves: he was Tom Norris, an Air Force F105 pilot, a Thud driver. (They called them "Thuds" because that's the noise they made when they hit the ground.) Tom had been shot down a month earlier than I.

As we compared stories, we discovered that we had been through almost identical experiences of interrogation, beating, and torture. Neither of us had been able to resist, and we were both greatly depressed over our performance. In a perverse way, it was quite comforting. Now, if we couldn't go home and face people when this was over, at least we could bum around with each other. We understood.

We had no contact with anyone else. We tried to see who was using the wash areas by peeking through a crack in the shuttered window. The guards patrolled the walkway and were constantly trying to catch us peeking, having made it very clear that we would be beaten if caught. One day while I was peeking through the crack, two Americans were brought to the wash area across from our cell. We finally would see more Americans. One I recognized immediately as Charlie Zuhoski, an F8 driver from my carrier, the *Oriskany*, who had been shot down in July 1967. Small world!

After a month Tom and I were moved to the "Thunderbird," another building in Las Vegas, and into a cell with two other Americans. One was Wally Newcomb, an Air Force F4 co-pilot or "GIB" (Guy in Back). The other was Charlie Zuhoski, the F8 driver from my ship.

We called our cells "rooms." We had rooms, not cells, and roommates, not cellmates. That was our own bit of psychological warfare. This room was about the same size as our previous one. The bedboards were stacked bunk-bed fashion. They had shackles at the foot — two iron bars. The bottom bar was fixed to the bed board. The top bar could be raised and your ankles put between the bars where they had been bent to accommodate them. The top bar could then be lowered and padlocked to the bottom bar. We hoped never to try them on for size.

The four of us sat for hours on the lower bunks, talking. All four of us had had similar "Welcome to Hanoi" experiences. Doing one's best was clearly taking shape in my mind as the only acceptable alternative to being superman.

We devised a mousetrap by propping up an old rice basket with a twig. A thread from a blanket was tied to the twig and allowed us to trigger the trap. We put a little rice under the basket, and for hours on end we caught and released the same little mouse over and over again. We had no contact with anyone else.

A week later, during the midafternoon siesta time, there was a lot of activity in the hallway, with doors opening and closing. Our door opened; we were told to roll up our stuff, blindfolded, and led to a truck. There were several other Americans on it already. We were seated apart from each other. When we tried to talk to each other we were hit and told to "kipsilem" (keep silent). The ride was short, an hour or so. We were unloaded and led to other cells. When the blindfolds were finally removed, Charlie and I were in a large room, about twenty feet square. There were two other Americans in it: Glenn Myers and Dennis Chambers, both Air Force F4 GIBs.

After introductions, we surveyed the situation. The room was big; on one side was a huge heavy door. In the wall opposite the door was a small barred and shuttered window at about waist height. The floor was made of reddish tiles a foot square. Along the floor on each of three sides were two small air vents sunk in cutouts below floor level. The ceiling was only about eight feet high. It had four 2-foot round air vents cut into it; these had been closed with barbed wire which was nailed down from above. Above the ceiling, the roof was made of slanted reddish tiles.

Outside our door was a walled wash area, roughly ten feet by eight. Its door was opposite the door of the room. As you walked out of the room into the wash area, to the far left was a cistern, with a bucket on a rope for drawing water. To the immediate left was a small brick room raised up about four steps. That was the "one-holer" toilet, built above its own holding tank.

As we came out the room door, to the right, along the outside wall of the room itself, was a ledge with a small roof over it. Here we kept our bowls and spoons. We could tell from studying the roofline that the building extended to our right, facing outward, but did not extend to our left.

This would be my home for the next year and a half. We would learn six months later that there were eight buildings here, each with two rooms. This prison was called the "Annex to the Zoo," the Zoo being a larger POW prison that ran along the other side of one wall of the Annex.

We were thrilled to be together and immediately started talking, introducing ourselves, telling our life histories. Whenever we talked in a normal tone of voice, the guards outside would yell at us, "Kipsilem." Several times they opened the door and along with the yelling administered a beating as punishment. We learned, quite quickly, to whisper. We whispered for the next six months. In a whisper, we told the story of how we were shot down, how we were welcomed to Hanoi — surprisingly similar stories. We told each other our histories, about our families, childhood stories; about books we had read, movies we had seen; we argued. We did it all in whispers.

Our daily routine was established by the clanging of the "gong," a long piece of metal that was hung up and then beaten with an iron rod. The clanging of the gong marked the passage of our days. I can describe my time in North Vietnamese prisons the same way many pilots describe flying: "Hours and hours of sheer boredom interspersed by moments of sheer terror." We spent the vast majority of our time locked up in rooms. If I were to describe in detail all of the terrible things that happened to me, I could account for only some handfuls of days out of five and a half years. If I were to describe in great detail all the terrible things that happened to American POWs in North Vietnam, I could account for a handful of years out of hundreds and hundreds of man-years. Mostly we had to deal with being locked up, and with the snail-slow passage of time.

Just before dawn, somewhere over in the Zoo, the gong would ring. That was the "get up" gong. We would arise and start our day. Soon after arriving in the Annex, we began to exercise: immediately after taking down our mosquito nets, we would do calisthenics. As our bodies recovered from the initial torture, we did sit-ups, push-ups, stretches, squats, jumping jacks: we knew that it was very important for us to take care of ourselves as best we could.

Later during our captivity, during the years when the Olympics were held, we would hold our own Olympic competitions. The record for push-ups was over one thousand; for sit-ups, over four thousand. Although we were skinny, we were in pretty good shape.

Probably around eight in the morning the "turnkey" — which was what we called the guard who opened and closed our doors — would arrive. The first chore of the day was for one of us to be let out to empty the bucket that served as our indoor toilet. We emptied it in the small brick building that was our outdoor toilet in the wash area and rinsed it with water drawn from the cistern. We had been given sandals with soles made from the tread of a car tire and straps made from an inner tube; these sandals made excellent toilet seats for the edge of the bucket.

After emptying the bucket, we placed our water pots on the shelf outside the room to the right. The turnkey then locked us back in the room and quite often gave us a ration of two North Vietnamese cigarettes, which must have been the brand made from the floor sweepings. They were really strong. Most of us considered smoking desirable; it was the only vice available to us, and those cigarettes were one of our only pleasures. The turnkey controlled the fire, so we were at his mercy for a light.

Pacing became the pastime of choice. We walked many hundreds of miles, pacing back and forth in those rooms. Around midmorning the first meal of the day arrived, along with boiled drinking water for our crock pots.

Almost invariably we were fed twice a day. Meals always consisted of a bowl of soup and either a bowl of rice or a hunk of a heavy, slightly dark French bread. During pumpkin season, we would have pumpkin soup twice a day for several months; during cabbage season, it was cabbage soup twice a day. Other less identifiable soups we had to give names, like sewer green soup, gasoline weeds, and morning glory soup.

On occasion there would be a little fatback in the soup. Sometimes we were given a side dish of some sort of vegetable, and on rare occasions some fish or meat. The fish was usually a bony little fish that had been dried in the sun, pulverized, heavily salted, and marinated with some kind of sauce. The meat might be fatback, buffalo, or dog. Rarely, an orange or "monkey banana" rounded out the menu.

Over the next few months my weight went from one hundred eighty to about one hundred twenty-five pounds. However, the diet would sustain that weight, even with vigorous daily calisthenics. We realized that, barring some drastic change in our treatment, we were not going to starve to death. We just were not going to be carrying a lot of excess weight around.

Around midmorning, the Vietnamese kitchen personnel would arrive with the first meal of the day. They carried it on a shoulder pole with a huge basket of bread or rice hanging from one end and a very large bucket of soup hanging from the other end. They would ladle the soup and rice into our bowls and leave. After the meal was served, the turnkey would open our door and we would take it into the room to eat. He, along with the food server, would then proceed to the next room. One by one, each room went through the routine. We were not allowed even to see any Americans except our own roommates.

The "siesta gong" was rung shortly after noon. Sometimes the turnkey would have come back around and let one of us out to wash the dishes prior to siesta, and sometimes that would happen later. The siesta lasted from two to three hours; we spent it sleeping, pacing, or talking quietly.

The gong that signaled the end of siesta sounded around three o'clock. Within an hour, the turnkey and the food server would be around with the second meal of the day, which was almost always identical to the first. By four or five we would be locked up for the rest of the day. The "go to bed gong" sounded around nine p.m., and we would string up our mosquito nets and crawl under them into our beds.

That routine went on with mind-numbing regularity, day after day, week after week, month after month, year after year. Anything outside the routine usually was not a good sign. One of the worst possible things was to hear the keys jingling at a non-routine time. That usually meant someone was going to interrogation, which we called a "quiz," and quizzes often led to beatings, which sometimes led to torture. We wanted to hear the keys only at the prescribed times. We became creatures of habit, and the routine was a great comfort.

Several annual events took place. Early in the war the American POWs had somehow convinced the Vietnamese (whom we called the "V" for short) that Christmas was a big deal. If they were really going to give us the "lenient and humane treatment" they always bragged about, that should include a Christmas celebration. Incredibly, the V bought into that. At Christmas we would have a special meal, with meat, vegetables, usually a piece of fruit, and a few pieces of candy. Many years they gave us a little rice wine at Christmas — enough for each of us to have a sip. The rice wine always provoked a lengthy discussion about whether we should each drink our own sip, or pool the rice wine and draw straws for the whole amount to see if someone could get a buzz on. Then, not to be outdone, the V provided an even more spectacular meal at Tet, when they celebrated the lunar New Year.

The first Christmas I had ever been away from my family I passed in December 1967 in that room in the Annex, with Charlie, Glenn, and Dennis. That year we described to each other, in all the detail we could muster, what Christmases had been like with our families when we were growing up. We were especially lavish with the details of Christmas dinner. There was not a dry eye in the room.

By that time we had received all of the standard issue of POW gear from our captors. Along with the mosquito net (one does not live without a mosquito net in Vietnam) and the sandals/toilet seat; we had a blanket (later, in the early 1970s, two blankets); a rice straw mat to sleep on; a tin cup; a bowl; a spoon; the small ceramic water pot, filled twice a day with boiled water; a towel about the size of a dish towel; two sets of shorts and T-shirts; one or two sets of long prison pants and long-sleeved shirts; soap; a V toothbrush; and V toothpaste. We were also supplied with toilet paper. It came in two-foot-square sheets that we tore into strips. It was a very coarse, brown material that barely qualified as paper.

The toothpaste was terrible. The best thing about it was that the toothpaste tube must have been almost pure lead, because we could write with it. Probably the worst thing we did to our health there was using the toothpaste that came out of that lead tube. We didn't have any paper except the toilet paper, which made fine, if very fragile, note paper.

We were not treated in accordance with any agreements on the treatment of prisoners of war — not the Geneva Accords, nor any other international laws governing the treatment of captured military personnel. We were interrogated on occasion, beaten on rare occasions, and tortured on very rare occasions.

Six months of our lives passed — very slowly, but passed nonetheless. The four of us learned everything about one another and had long discussions on every conceivable topic. The longest of those revolved around how many Oreo cookies we really, truly thought we could actually eat, with and without ice cream. We were a bit preoccupied with the subject of food.

4

On Becoming a Professional POW

In mid-April, during siesta, we could hear a lot of activity in the Annex — at the wrong time for activity. The door opened and four more Americans were moved in. The door closed. We thought we had gone to heaven. Whispering, we began to introduce ourselves. Two of our new roommates had been in Hanoi at least a year longer than any of us had. One of them, Tom McNish, said in a normal tone of voice — which sounded like shouting to us — "Why are you whispering?" We told him, "Shhh, if they hear you we'll be in trouble, someone will get beaten."

I'll never forget the incredulous look on Tom's face. He said, "Are you guys nuts? Do you really think they have enough guards to go around to all of these rooms listening and beating people for talking normally? You'll only get in trouble if you make a lot of noise." We quit whispering.

The very next thing Tom asked was, "Who are you in touch with? Who lives next door?" We just gaped at him. We weren't "in touch" with anyone. Who lived next door? How the hell should we know? How do you get "in touch"?

Tom was really disgusted with us. Telling us to watch from the cracks in the doors and windows for guards, he went to the common wall between the two rooms and began tapping. In moments he knew who was next door, and they were working on getting in touch with the other buildings and finding out who was living in the Annex, and who the senior ranking officer was.

Charlie, Dennis, Glenn and I were speechless. These guys knew everything. There was a whole covert communications network in place here; POWs were organized; we had a chain of command; POWs were actively supporting each other. It was wonderful. I count that afternoon as the time I became a professional POW. We set about learning everything from our new roommates.

First, we learned the tap code. Tom had gone over to the wall and tapped a rhythm every American instantly recognizes as "shave and a haircut," to which any American responds automatically "two bits," or "tap tap." That was the test to be certain that our contacts in the next cell were Americans and not our captors sneaking around trying to catch us communicating. Americans recognize and replicate that rhythm instantaneously — probably the influence of years of watching "Looney Tunes."

Our captors knew what we were doing. They beat it out of us. Then they would sneak around trying to tap to us on the wall so they could catch us breaking their rules. However, they could never replicate that rhythm. They didn't have "Looney Tunes" in that country.

The code Tom was tapping was a 5 x 5 matrix into which all of the letters of the alphabet were placed. Someone had devised it based on an idea he remembered from a Russian novel about prisoners. The matrix looked like this:

	1	2	3	4	5
1	A	F	L	Q	V
2	B	G	M	R	W
3	C	H	N	S	X
4	D	I	O	T	Y
5	E	J	P	U	Z

Because there are twenty-six letters in our alphabet and only twenty-five squares in the matrix, we used the letter C for K.

We could then tap a number from the horizontal axis and one from the vertical, thus locating a letter in the matrix. For example: One-one (tap-tap) was the letter A; one-two (tap, tap-tap) was B; one-three (tap, tap-tap-tap) was C, and so on.

We all became very proficient with that code. At times, if you put your ear to the wall, it clattered like a high-school typing class just before graduation. That code was so good, we used it for everything. If the guards took us out, gave us the bamboo broom, and told us to sweep down the walkway in between the buildings, we would sweep in the code: swish swish (pause) swish swish swish (H); (pause) (pause) swish swish (pause) swish swish swish swish (I). It was like being on the radio. Everyone listened. We could tell jokes and send whatever information we wished, right under the noses of our captors.

If the guards took us out without the broom, we would communicate with body noises — not the kind of body noises you might imagine! We would cough and spit, clear our throats and hack. Cough (pause) spit hack spit (H); (pause pause) spit hack (pause) cough cough cough spit (I).

Sometimes with new guys we had to start the communications process by tapping one tap for the letter A, two taps for B, three taps for C, and so on. The process was

repeated until the neophyte on the other side of the wall
caught on. He wanted desperately to communicate, so it was
relatively easy to figure out that the tapping sequence was
taking him through the alphabet. We Navy personnel had to
start out very simply, because some of these guys were in
the Marine Corps. Some were even in the Air Force.

There were numerous other ways we were able to
communicate. We developed a one-handed gestural
alphabet for communicating on the rare occasions we
were able to see each other at close range, and a two-
handed alphabet for communicating at longer range. If we
had a crack in the doors or shutters across which we could
flash, we could use Morse code, which we had all learned
as aviators; all the navigational aids in aviation are iden-
tified in Morse code. We didn't take the time to use Morse
code for tapping on the walls because the matrix code was
more efficient.

I mentioned writing with the toothpaste tubes; we also
made an ink from ashes and dirt. We were let out to wash
several times a week. In most prisons other than the Annex,
the wash areas were used in common by various Americans,
one room at a time. Those wash areas were favorite places to
drop notes for whoever would be next to use the wash area.

For the four of us, it was nothing short of a miracle to
find out that we were organized; that we were able to
support each other on a scale larger than a few people in one
room; and that those who were senior really were in charge.
The down side was learning how brutal the treatment really
had been — all of the torture and beatings that had gone on
and were still continuing.

We learned that priority one was always communication. First and foremost, we all had to be in contact with one
another. We quickly devised ways to communicate between
the buildings. For example, there was a slight crack under
the door from the walkway into our wash area. Across the

walkway in the next building, someone could stick his head down into the ventilation hole, which was below the level of the floor. He could then watch the crack under our door. We would flash code and he could copy, and then the process could be reversed. Before long, all the buildings in the Annex were in constant communication.

Of course, we didn't all learn all these communications procedures at the same time or in the same way. However, once we managed to make contact with any new guy, teaching him how to communicate was always the first priority. Soon everyone in each prison knew who was there; who was senior; what was going on in the other rooms; who was being interrogated; what the V officers were asking for; and what our senior officer wanted us to say or do.

All this was not without risk. The V were very serious about keeping us isolated. They regularly tried to catch us communicating, and being caught meant receiving a beating. So all of our communications were covert, very secretive. When one roommate was tapping on the wall, all the others were on lookout for guards, eyes pressed to the cracks in the shutters, ears to the floor listening for footsteps. We were in this together and taking care of each other.

Eight people in a room was awesome. We had much to tell and teach one another, so passing the time became somewhat easier.

We began to schedule regular "movie" nights. Typically we had a room meeting to work out the entertainment schedule. (We always had 100 percent attendance at our meetings.) We would discuss movies and books. It was enough for someone to say that he had seen a particular movie or read a certain book. We would immediately schedule him to tell us that story — that night, next week, next month, six months from now, next year. We were really into long-range planning in those prisons.

The newly appointed storyteller would first talk to all his roommates to find out everything anybody knew about his chosen movie or book. He would then tap a message on the wall, sending an inquiry around the prison. Eventually he knew everything that anyone knew about that movie or book. Then he could sit in a corner for as long as he wanted and fill in all the blank spots in the story. When the scheduled night arrived, we would sprawl on the concrete floor while he told us the story.

Over the years we became very proficient at storytelling. I even received an Academy Award — for *Dr. Zhivago*. After I had been there for a number of years, moved from cell to cell and prison to prison, in December 1970 I was moved in with a group of twenty men at a prison we would eventually call Unity. My reputation preceded me. They wanted to know, "When can you tell us *Zhivago?*" We scheduled it for Sunday night — Sunday Night at the Movies.

I appointed a sound team of three men, who sat to one side; whenever I nodded my head, they would start singing "Lara's Theme" from the movie. I told *Zhivago* in the first person, as though I were Alec Guiness, the brother, out searching for the lost daughter. It took me five and a half hours to tell the whole story. As I concluded, there was a spontaneous standing ovation. My cellmates awarded me the Oscar on the spot!

About once a week the turnkey would bring us a razor so we could shave when we washed. The kicker was that we would only get one new razor blade for all eight of us, if we were lucky. It was tough shaving with only cold water and soap, especially if you were number eight (or higher) on the blade. So I decided to grow a goatee; I didn't really have much else to do. It seemed like a good idea at the time.

After several weeks my goatee was beginning to look pretty good. The turnkey kept glancing at it kind of funny but never said anything about it. One day the turnkey, an officer, and several guards entered our wash area. The turnkey unlocked the door and called me out, locking the door behind me. I was told to kneel down in the wash area.

Kneeling was one of their ways of punishing us for infractions of their rules. They would make us kneel for hours on the concrete or brick floors. If we refused, they would beat us until we were kneeling. So the choices were kneel, or be beaten and kneel. I knelt. The guards proceeded to take turns hitting and kicking me.

After they worked me over pretty well, the officer told me to shave: I was not permitted to grow a beard. Besides being mad about getting a beating, I was furious that they had not simply told me to shave.

A little over a year passed. During that time there were occasional quizzes, but fortunately not much rough stuff. We could recite most of each other's life stories and knew which movies each man could tell.

Another of our coping mechanisms was laughter. It was the way that we kept some balance and perspective in our lives. Part of the prison complex in downtown Hanoi we called "Heartbreak Hotel." It consisted of eight cells, four on either side of a dark little corridor. Old cell number eight down at the end had been converted into a shower. They had run a rusty water pipe into it, up the wall, and bent it over up at the top. After a man's arrival in Hanoi, and when they were finished with him, sooner or later, maybe weeks later, the guards would come to take him to the shower in Heartbreak.

The guards would drag him, kick him, pull him, shove him, somehow get him down to old cell number eight. They would throw him into the cell, slamming the door behind him, and yell, "Wash!" He would stand there in whatever tattered rags he had left, usually hurting in body and spirit. When he finally got the water on, it felt so good, running down over his filthy, battered, bruised body. Sooner or later he had to look up, and right there at eye level, in the concrete, someone had scratched "Smile, you're on candid camera!"

Laughter was the way we coped with the pressure. Laughter was the way we kept our sanity, held everything together. It was the way we let off the pressure, tried to keep things in perspective, maintained our balance.

We had one fellow who went to interrogation one day. The interrogator wanted to know, "In your country, where do your parents live?" He told them, "Kansas." The interrogator said, "Your parents, what do they do?" He told him, "They are farmers." The interrogator then asked, "What do your parents grow?" He told him, "They grow updoc." Later on that day, the interrogator took him back to his cell.

Then the interrogator went to another cell. The little spy door opened with a bang, and there stood the man we called the Elf. He wanted to know, "What's updoc? What's updoc? What's updoc?"

It didn't make any sense at all. Everyone was thinking the Elf had popped his cork. But he really wanted to know: "What's updoc?" He was standing there with his face pressed in that little trap door, and he was really starting to get excited. The veins were standing out in his forehead. He was starting to scream and sputter. "What's updoc?"

Everyone was thinking, "Oh please, give us a hint, give us a hint." Finally the Elf screamed, "You know! Updoc! Grows on farm in Kansas!"

Ah! Yes, of course, updoc! So they told him, "It's about five feet high when it matures. Updoc looks a lot like maize … it has a red flower on it that grows into a yellow gourd-like vegetable … we use it in soups."

He wanted to know everything about updoc. So they taught him everything there is to know about it. They taught him the recipe for updoc bread, and even the Latin name for updoc.

There was another prison we named Alcatraz. It was a series of twelve one-man cells. When Americans were in Alcatraz, they lived alone and were generally kept in leg irons twenty-four hours a day. (Picture a steel horseshoe-shaped shackle over each ankle, with a bar going through the shackles behind the ankles.)

One day the guards at Alcatraz decided they were going to have the Americans wash out their cells. They went around and took everyone's leg irons off and threw them in a pile in the courtyard. Then they started with the American in the first cell, took him out, drew water, and had him wash out his cell. The guards then proceeded to the next cell. By the end of the day, all the cells were washed out.

The turnkey then went to the pile of leg irons, grabbed the nearest set, and went into the closest cell. The American who was in there insisted, "Those are not my leg irons. I am not putting those things on. I want my leg irons!" The guard, who didn't speak English, had no idea what to do.

Soon there were three or four guards running all over Alcatraz with handfuls of leg irons that no one would put on, insisting that they weren't their own. Well, of course, the guards solved that problem in their own inimitable way: they began forcibly putting the leg irons on in whatever order suited them.

The next day, the senior American POW at Alcatraz, reflecting on what had happened, tapped a message to the rest of the fellows there. What he said was, "When we go back to the United States, I don't think any of us should talk to the shrinks."

Maybe we were all a little crazy. But we were laughing.

One of the POWs had a cockroach. Yes, a cockroach. He had built a chariot for his cockroach. He was concerned that one day there would be an announcement that we were going to have cockroach chariot races. So every day he would get his cockroach out, put the chariot on it, and run it around in a circle in the middle of his cell. If there were going to be cockroach chariot races, he wanted his cockroach to be in shape. He was training it.

One day, during a training session, the inevitable happened. The cockroach got out of the loop, went under the door, and was gone. Now, picture the guy on the other side of the wall. The message that comes tapping through says: "Have you seen a cockroach pulling a chariot?"

5

Hot Poop Red

In May of 1969, we had two POWs from the Annex escape. It had been a long time in the planning. We had discovered that we could work the barbed wire in the ceiling ventilation holes loose and thus get up in the attics of the buildings. From there we could push roof tiles up and peek out beyond the walls of the Annex. We all reported what we could see over the walls behind our buildings. The escape had been planned and debated for quite a while. In the discussions of the pros and cons of trying to escape, there were plenty of us on either side.

The argument against trying to escape went as follows. It was impossible to escape and go unnoticed in the area surrounding Hanoi. There were one thousand V per square foot in the Hanoi area. And everybody there was Vietnamese. All of us were taller than the V and none of us looked like them. The recurring plan was a very long shot: to get into the river, then float down it to Haiphong, on through the harbor, and out into the Gulf of Tonkin, where one might eventually be picked up by a passing U.S. Navy warship.

Once in the prison system, no one had ever been successful in escaping for more than a few hours. Escape attempts always brought an increase in beatings and torture. It wasn't worth it.

Then there was the argument in favor. First, the military Code of Conduct dictated, "I will make every attempt to escape and aid others to escape." It didn't make any provision for weighing the odds of success. Second, with a successful escape, the brutality of our treatment would be exposed, and surely that would cause public outrage, putting pressure on the V to improve our treatment. Even though it was a long shot, it was worth the risk.

I personally had very ambivalent feelings about the whole idea, and in the end was not in favor of it.

As part of the planning process, all of us in the Annex were told that if it were possible when the escape took place, we would all be notified through the communications network. The code words indicating that the escapees had gone were "hot poop red."

The idea, the planning, and the debate went on until sometime in the spring of 1969 when we were told to forget it. The room planning the escape was the same room in which the Senior Ranking Officer (SRO) for the Annex lived. They had decided against it.

Several weeks later, on a Sunday morning — May 11, 1969 — the turnkey was very edgy when he let us out to dump the buckets. While we were out, we managed to pick up a message from the room across the walkway. The message was "hot poop red." In spite of the plan having been canceled, the two escapees had gone out early Sunday morning in a driving rainstorm. The temptation to escape, after all the previous planning and debate, had been too great. The two had gone through the ceiling and over the wall sometime after midnight.

They were captured about daybreak and brought back into the Zoo, having been loose for only a few hours. That escape attempt resulted in a purge and the most brutal round of torture in Vietnam POW history. The two who had escaped were moved to Hoa Lo, put in leg irons, severely beaten, and tortured. One of them did not survive.

Meanwhile, back at the Annex, the SRO from each room was taken out and beaten. The SRO for the Annex was beaten and tortured. This systematic beating was also conducted with a vengeance in the Zoo itself. Probably the gravest error committed in the Annex was not consulting and getting permission for the escape from the SRO in the Zoo. Therefore, the SRO and others in the Zoo had no idea what caused the beatings and torture they were enduring.

Altogether, nearly thirty Americans were beaten and tortured. The "ropes" were no longer the preferred method of torture. Beatings were administered with a rubber strap that we recognized as a fan belt from an automobile. A man was made to lie down on his stomach with trousers down and no shirt. The guards would then beat him across the back, buttocks, and thighs.

Within days, the guards had boarded up all of the ventilation holes in the ceilings, as well as those along the edges of the floors. The already terrible heat and humidity became worse. Everyone had severe heat rash. The most horrible thing, though, was that we could hear the V beating and flaying our buddies. There was nothing we could do but listen, and weep, and pray. The beatings went on for several months that summer.

In August of 1969 there was another room shuffle. I ended up in the room across the walkway with several new roommates. The purge was fading and we began settling back into the routine.

One day later that fall, we heard the keys jingling at the wrong time. The turnkey opened the door and called

John Borling and me out of the room. Guards led us off to two different quiz rooms. An interrogator, the Elf, began to go back and forth between us, interrogating us one at a time. He claimed that a guard listening outside our cell door had heard us talking about things we were not allowed to discuss.

The interrogations went on for several days, eventually leading to beatings and torture. We were made to lie on our stomachs on the floor, no shirt, pants down to our ankles, and were beaten with the fan belt. The guard stood back and took several steps toward me, whipping the fan belt from behind his back in an arc, bringing it down across my back, flaying the skin off and turning the back of my body into hamburger. The impact was so hard that my body bounced off the floor and quivered with pain. The Elf really wanted us to tell him what we were talking about.

The Elf insisted we were talking about something forbidden. Neither John nor I had any idea what he was after. The beatings continued, with the Elf going back and forth between John and me in our separate cells. After several lashes, the Elf would ask us what we were talking about. We both told him, "About my father, the truck driver." (In fact, we had been talking about my father, who was a truck driver.) It became obvious that the Elf was serious about this, and we couldn't figure out what the hell he wanted.

After several days and numerous beatings, the Elf said to each of us separately, "What about the escape plan?" Ah! So that's what he was after! Well, we were not dummies, and we were hurting badly enough to be desperate to stop the beatings.

So each of us said to him, "Oh yes, we discussed the escape plan." The Elf began writing in his notebook. We had confessed to planning an escape. The exact same scenario went on with both John and me.

Of course, our escape plans had to be identical. The Elf began systematically going back and forth between the two of us, extracting the escape plan. The process was to have one of us beaten for several lashes and then to feed us part of the plan, line by line. For example, he would ask, "How did you plan to get over the wall?" I said, trying to think as fast as I could through the pain, "We were going to get on the roof of the cook shack and then go over the wall."

The Elf would say, "What about the blanket?" Blanket? I'm thinking to myself, blanket? "Oh yes, we were going to throw the blanket over the barbed wire on the top of the wall so we could get over it without getting caught or cut!" He wrote that down in his little notebook, then he would go to John and repeat the process.

Step by step, the Elf beat the same story out of both of us, until finally he had written identical escape plans in his notebook. It was insane, but the Elf had what he wanted: our escape plan. It would have been comical if it hadn't hurt so much.

The second thing the Elf was after, when he had beaten us sufficiently to loosen our tongues, was to find out what the POWs were collectively up to and what new orders the SROs had given following the escape attempt in May. In fact, the V had been so vigorous in their attempts to close down the communications system that not much of anything was being communicated. Since they were simultaneously beating the same information out of John and me, they were inclined to believe we were telling them the truth — fortunately for us.

The beating and story extraction took a couple of weeks. John and I then spent four weeks in solitary confinement (we called it "solo"). So it was about six weeks later when the guards dumped the two of us back into the room from which they had taken us. Our roommates wanted to know what had happened. John and I told them the entire story. It was clear to us that major problems could result from the V listening outside the doors, not understanding English very well, and beating us for what they thought we were saying.

We came to the only logical conclusion: we must quit speaking English. What we decided to speak was Pig Latin. We set aside an entire evening to review the rules for the grammatical construction of Pig Latin; that takes about one minute. The next morning, at the crack of dawn, we started speaking nothing but Pig Latin. We soon learned that it takes about four hours of speaking nothing but Pig Latin until you begin to go stark raving mad.

In the middle of those four hours, I let slip the fact that I had studied French for two years in high school and two years at the Naval Academy. My roommates, who were going crazy trying to speak Pig Latin, decided that we should immediately shift to French. It didn't matter that I hadn't learned anything in those four years. I had to tap a message on the wall and send it around the prison: "I am now the French professor. Anybody who knows any French words, send them over here. I need some vocabulary." And so I started to teach French.

I taught French for years. When older V officers occasionally came around, I used to hit them up for help, since many of them had learned French during the French occupation of Indochina. I would say, in French, "I'm the French professor. How do you say...." They would always puff up a little bit and teach the stupid American some French.

So I taught French for years. By the time we came back to the United States, I had six men absolutely fluent in the French language — according to me. It was a little drifty, and I had to make some things up. But oh, how we could speak it!

Actually, it was a little more solid than that. On a couple of occasions, the V let me see a magazine in French, and once they gave me a third-year university French textbook printed in Moscow. The only problem with it was that it was entirely in French. I had it for about a month. I devoured it, and what I couldn't figure out I made up. On our return to the United States, two of my students took tests and received college credit for their French. In addition to French, other POWs taught Spanish, German, and a smattering of several other languages.

For a short time we were given some paper and colored pencils. The V told us we would be allowed to draw. We sent a message to the SRO of the Annex, who forwarded it to the SRO in the Zoo. We asked whether we could use the materials, and if yes, for guidance as to what we could do with them. We were concerned that the V would take advantage of anything we did to portray our treatment falsely. They always bragged to us about how leniently and humanely we were being treated, despite the fact that deprivation, interrogations, beatings and torture were the rule. We knew that there would be no way to bring any pressure to bear on the V if the world thought we were being treated reasonably.

The response came back from the SRO that we could use the materials so long as we didn't do anything that could be construed as political or having anything to do with the war. We were delighted. Real pencils, real paper, we could hardly believe it. We experimented drawing fish and birds — very innocuous subjects. After a few weeks, the materials were taken from us.

I discovered after I was released that several drawings did eventually make it to my family via some antiwar delegation from eastern Europe. My family was delighted. I was not. It gave them a false sense of how we were really being treated. We were never successful in our quest to be treated in accordance with international law and the Geneva Conventions.

In the fall of 1969 there was a slight change in our treatment that in time would herald larger and more favorable changes. Before that, it had been pretty much open season on Americans. If the turnkeys or guards felt like knocking us around, they did. If the V wanted something, there was a recognizable progression to the interrogation process: questions, threats, beatings, torture. We all knew the pattern.

They knew they could eventually get whatever they wanted from us, or make us do anything. We were determined that whatever they wanted, they would have to take forcibly. We would give them nothing. They knew that too. Each side had established very good credibility with the other.

After the fall of 1969, the turnkeys and guards were no longer permitted to knock us around whenever they felt like it. They never touched us again without being ordered to do so. In fact, even the interrogators had to get permission to work us over. At quiz the recognizable progression would begin, but when it got to the point where the rough stuff started, there would be a time-out. The interrogator would leave, and it became apparent to us after a while that he had to go and get permission to proceed. Sometimes he would return with permission, and sometimes he wouldn't return at all. After we sat there for a few hours, a guard would take us back to our cell. As the years passed, the interrogator would return with permission less and less often.

It wasn't much of a change, but for us it made a huge difference. It was very, very difficult to live under the constant threat of physical punishment. If we heard the keys at a time when they were not scheduled, our stomachs would churn, our palms would sweat. The pressure was unreal. The changes in fall of 1969 took away some of that constant pressure.

There were probably several reasons for that change. One was that Ho Chi Minh had died in September. From what I've read, that had a significant impact. Evidently his administration had a lot to do with the harsh brutality of our treatment.

Another factor was the beginning of the POW/MIA movement on our behalf in the United States. Our families could no longer keep silent about us. Letter-writing campaigns to the Hanoi government were organized to express concern over how we were being treated. The National League of Families of POW/MIAs was organized. People began wearing bracelets engraved with our names and the dates we were shot down. Ross Perot had an aircraft flying all over the Orient trying to deliver CARE packages to us.

I believe all these activities led the V to the realization that we might be worth something to them someday. As a result, they made slight changes in our treatment. They removed the constant threat of physical violence.

They also decided that we would be permitted to write our families. Almost two and a half years after I was shot down, my family learned that I was still alive. Until then, they had known only that I had been alive when I reached the ground and had talked with Dean when he flew over.

A fellow POW and good friend of mine from flight training, Bill Metzger, wrote one of the first letters — to his wife, Bonnie. In the letter, Bill said, "Tell Uncle Dave that I will look forward to seeing him again any Wednesday." Any Wednesday was the name of a play that Bill, Bonnie, another couple, and I had attended at the Old Globe Theater in San Diego just a few days before Bill left for Vietnam. Bonnie immediately knew that Bill was telling her that I was alive, and she conveyed that to my family.

Later I too was permitted to write to my family. The writing was restrictive and heavily censored. The guards would take us to quiz and place in front of us an eight-by-six-inch form. The top half was a box with seven lines in it, about the size of a postcard. The bottom half had printed instructions for writing and sending letters to us in North Vietnam.

Our letters had to be written on those seven lines. We would write as small as possible in order to get as much as we could into those few lines. Then we would be taken back to our room, and they would take the letter to be censored.

Hours, days, or weeks later — or often, not at all — the turnkey would fetch us back to the quiz room. We would be given the censored draft and a new, clean form. We were to copy the censored letter exactly onto the new form. What they censored didn't necessarily make any sense. Sometimes they would block out random verbs or adjectives. Often the resulting sentences weren't grammatical or didn't make sense. However, if we didn't copy it precisely, the letter was immediately trashed. We quickly learned that anything we wrote had to be very bland.

6

Karen's Waiting

One day at a quiz, the V officer seemed to be in a good mood. I told him that if I were allowed to write a letter again, I wanted to write to my sweetheart. "You have a sweetheart?" he grunted. The he turned his little notebook around on the table and said, "Write the name and address of your sweetheart here." I wrote Karen's name and address down in his book.

Some months later, I did have an opportunity to write again. It was a different prison and a different presiding officer. I told him, "This time I will write to my sweetheart; the other officer said it would be allowed." Then I quickly put my head down without waiting for an answer and started to write. For whatever reason, it worked. Over the last couple of years, I was able to write occasionally to Karen.

After that time in early 1970, I wrote alternately to my family and to Karen — a total of fifteen or twenty letters over three years. I also received ten or fifteen letters from Karen and my family. The lag time between when letters were written and when we received them was months.

Many families had been writing all along — we just never received those letters.

Karen and I had met in January of 1967 on a blind date arranged by my roommate's fiancée, who was Karen's sorority sister. It was love at first sight. All these years later, I can remember every detail of that first date. During the next five months before the *Oriskany* left for Vietnam, Karen and I were together every possible moment.

Karen graduated from San Jose State University in January of 1967 and was living with her parents. She had been accepted as a flight attendant with United Airlines, but during her physical, the doctor discovered a lump in her right breast. The lump turned out to be benign, but having it removed caused her to put off her flight attendant class until after I was to leave in June. By the time June rolled around, we had become so serious that Karen decided it would not be fair to go to work for United, only to leave eight months later to marry me when I returned from cruise.

Before I left, I told Karen that if anything happened to me, I would like her to connect with my family in Pennsylvania. I had introduced her to them over the telephone, but I wanted her to meet them in person. I thought that in tragic circumstances they would be very good for each other.

Several months after I was shot down, Karen called my parents and asked if she might come back to Pennsylvania for a visit. They were delighted. She fell in love with them, and they with her. Over the five and a half years I was in prison, she made nine trips back east to visit them. She became very close to my parents — closer to them than she ever would have been had I not been shot down and out of the picture for so long.

My father died in the fall of 1969. We noticed that in early letters from my family, my mother talked about my father and signed, "Love, Mom and Dad." Later, though, she stopped mentioning Dad, and the letters were signed, "Love, Mom." We deduced that my Dad had died. He had had a massive heart attack in the winter of 1964, following which he had recovered well but had never been able to return to work.

I have always been sorry that I didn't have the chance to spend more time with him. There were so many things I would like to have said to him. I was eighteen in 1960 when I left home to attend the Naval Academy. I had only been home for holidays and short visits since then. Dad and I had been close, hunting and fishing while I was growing up, but not nearly as close as I anticipated we would become in the future. Now it wouldn't be possible. Whenever I think that I never had a chance to say goodbye, or tell him how much I loved him, or that he will never see my children, it brings tears to my eyes.

From sometime in 1970 on, we even began to receive some photographs from our families. At first they just gave some of us a few pictures. Later, they sealed them in plastic before giving them to us. They were apparently afraid we were receiving microdots with who knows what information on them, somewhere in the pictures.

Early in 1969 we were allowed to receive occasional packages from our families. The packages were ransacked and searched for contraband, messages, or anything else not allowed. (It was more likely an excuse to pilfer items from the packages.) Over the next several years, most of us would occasionally receive a package. It was wonderful to have a little Kool-Aid, chewing gum, candy, or instant coffee on occasion.

During all those years in prison, I learned an enormous amount about myself. I learned that I'm okay. I had always thought so, but now I knew for sure. More

important than that, I found out that the vast majority of
people are okay. I learned that all the little things that
bother me, bother all of us. I had no idea before that this
was so.

I was locked up with men who were smart, educated,
and strong. I could pick any subject, think about it for as
long as I wanted to, and then I could go to these guys and
say, "This is what I've been thinking about. What is this like
with you?"

I found out that basically people are all the same.
However, our inclination is to see ourselves in isolation and
to spin our own cocoons around ourselves. The tendency is
to think, "I'm the only one who gets in these situations";
"I'm the only one who goes into a new group of people and
feels awkward, out of place"; "I'm the only one who can't
think of the right thing to say"; "I'm the only one who says
these stupid things, gets my foot this far in my mouth";
"I'm the only one that has to work with these kind of
turkeys."

It was reassuring to learn that people feel the same
and think the same in all these situations. I had been in
many conversations after which, as I was putting the key
in the ignition of my car, I would think of what I should
have said: the comment that would have dazzled
everyone. Now I learned that we're all the same — out in
the parking lot, starting our cars, thinking about what we
should have said!

Here's another example. I know that at least the men
reading this will be able to identify with it immediately.
When I was a bachelor. I would go out for a night on the
town; end up some place; belly up to the bar, and order a
drink. I'd look around and spot a young lady sitting across
the room. I'd start working on my lines.

Now, I am about to disclose some man stuff. The only
way men will let me get away with it is if I swear all the

women readers to secrecy. Here is the way it is with men; maybe it's the same with women — I don't know.

I'm leaning on the bar, having a drink, thinking, "She should meet me." I start working on my lines, and they're getting pretty good. This is going to be so smooth, she won't have a chance — I'll sweep her off her feet! Pretty soon I'm not only working on my lines for right now; I have them worked out for the entire weekend, or maybe even a week or two ahead.

Finally, I get my courage about as high as I can. I take a few deep breaths, being careful not to hyperventilate. I turn around to make my move — and there's some fellow over there talking to her.

I don't know what other guys did, or still do, in that situation, but I'd take myself out into the parking lot and kick myself around. "What's wrong with me?" I'd ask myself. "Look at him, look how smooth he is. Why can't I be like him? Instead here I am hanging on this bar, drinking this swill, making up these lines. Why can't I be like he is? What's the matter with me?"

Here is what I learned by talking with, and living with, other POWs in Hanoi: that other fellow started working on his lines half an hour before I did.

In this and in many other ways, I learned to be very comfortable with myself, and that was no easy feat. Before I was shot down, my life was going about a million miles an hour. On shore, it was go, go, go. At sea, it was fly, eat, sleep, fly, eat, sleep.

Then my million-mile-an-hour life came to a screeching halt. I found myself locked in a small room, about the size of a bed, with someone I didn't know — and that someone was me. Talk about scary! It took me months to be comfortable with myself, to be able to pick subjects and think about them in depth, to learn about myself.

Victor Frankel, an Austrian psychiatrist, was a Jew who was interned in Nazi concentration camps. He talks about the "existential vacuum," which he describes as our discomfort with ourselves. In this state, we find no meaning in our existence; we feel a constant uneasiness with ourselves, a constant need for activity and distraction in our lives. It manifests itself in our discomfort with quiet time and solitude.

The "Sunday neurosis" is an illustration. Imagine yourself at home alone on a Sunday afternoon. You decide to watch the football game on TV. You turn it on, but there's no game on — in fact, nothing of any interest. What's there to do? Ah, mow the lawn — no, the kid mowed it yesterday. I don't know what you do next, but about now most Americans head for the refrigerator.

Our existential vacuum is an inability to sit in a chair and think, to be content with ourselves, to be comfortable without distracting activity. In prison, it took me months to get comfortable with myself, but it was wonderful once I was able to relax and be at peace. If only I had had more faith back then — the faith that produces "the peace that passes all understanding."

I continue to be comfortable with myself, though, in all honesty, I must now force myself to sit in that chair. But after a half hour or so, I can settle in and begin to think in depth about my chosen topic.

In those cells I examined my life from as far back as I could remember to as far into the future as I could possibly imagine. I reordered the priorities in my life. Before being shot down, I had decided that I would do whatever I possibly could to spend my life flying from an aircraft carrier. Carrier aviation was the most fun, challenging, exciting, scary, rewarding, invigorating, and terrifying thing I had ever done. I had no use for an assignment that would take me off an aircraft carrier. If I could fly there, I would stay at sea for my entire life; there was nothing that could be any better. I had already been scheming how I might transfer from one carrier squadron to another.

Sitting around in prison thinking about it, though, I decided I wanted to marry: to marry Karen, if she waited. I wanted to have children someday, and to be a very active participant in their lives. I was not going to be an absentee parent. That series of decisions was incompatible with constantly being at sea on an aircraft carrier. So after my release and return to the United States, I had to restructure my Naval career. In fact, I never went back to sea again. My assignments and the squadrons I commanded were all at Naval Air Station Miramar in San Diego.

I changed in other ways too. Karen would have said I was much more sensitive and understanding, more able to communicate my feelings, more thoughtful, and more tolerant. Of course, she eventually gave all the credit to the marriage counseling class we had in Hanoi.

I found out that stress isn't entirely bad for us. Nowadays stress gets blamed for everything, and some of it is a bum rap. Sailing offers a good analogy. Stress is what makes a sailboat move through the water. It is the tension of the wind against the sail that produces movement. If there's not enough tension, there's no movement; too much tension, and the boat tips over.

7

Moved to the Zoo

Six of us were moved from the Annex into the "Office" in the Zoo in the fall of 1969. On one side of us was a cell with two men in it; the cell on the other side was empty. Farther down the building were two more cells, which were occupied. The only wash area for the whole building was in a corner of the Office courtyard. The turnkey would let us out one room at a time to wash and dump the buckets.

We had learned that in some buildings we could actually talk through the walls. If you put your cup bottom against the wall and sealed your mouth into the cup with your hands, you could talk into it and the cup muffled the sound. The listener on the other side of the wall located the exact spot by tapping, then placed the bottom of his cup against his ear and the mouth of the cup against the wall to listen. Sometimes we could use a blanket as a seal around our faces against the wall and talk that way.

We took it on ourselves to entertain the two guys next door. It was hard to live alone, and very difficult with only one roommate. One evening, we told them not to worry about watching for guards. We would do that. We asked them both to come and put their cups against the wall. Once we had them in listening position four of us put our heads very close together with our cups in the transmit position. We then put on a magnificent production of *Oklahoma* through the wall. We had raised POW entertainment to a new level.

During the dry season, the water in the well in the wash area sank very low. One day when we went out to clean up, we looked into the well to draw water with the bucket and saw, floating at the bottom of the well, a little dead fish. We couldn't imagine where it came from. Carefully we maneuvered the bucket under the fish and brought it up. Then we took a twig and stuck it to a small sapling growing in the corner of the wash area.

That day during siesta we bumped the entire building up on the back wall. If we wanted to tap to the guys next door, we would tap on the wall between the two rooms. If we wanted to tap to the entire building, we went to the back wall, and after a couple of good bumps on it to get everyone's attention, we were able to tap on the back wall and broadcast up and down the length of the building.

That day we sent a message to the entire building that went something like this: "As you all know, today is the last day of the Annual Fishing Derby. Don't act dumb. You know full well how hard the entertainment committee has been working to make certain that we all have fun on this camping trip. Many announcements have been made.

"If we are really going to have fun on this camping trip, we will all need to participate in some of these wonderful activities. The committee has been very sad to see that there is only one entry in the fishing derby posted on the sapling in the wash area. It is the kind of apathy you are all demonstrating that will really make this camping trip miserable, not only for yourselves but for everyone here. In fact it is this very same sort of apathy which, if it is allowed to progress, will be the ruin of a great nation like the United States.

"We want to encourage you to get in the swing of this camping trip and partake in the wonderful activities that the entertainment committee is planning. It is our sincere hope that you will see fit to get involved in the fishing derby this afternoon when you go out to wash your dishes after the evening meal. The prize ribbon for the winner of the fishing derby will be presented later today. There is still time to catch a lunker and go home a winner. Let's all have fun."

Then we got off the wall. We quickly took a piece of toilet paper and tore it into the shape of a prize ribbon. We darkened it a little with ashes. When we were let out to wash our dishes following the afternoon meal, we pinned the ribbon to our entry. That evening we bumped everyone in the building up on the back wall and announced the winner of the annual fishing derby. We gave them an extensive lecture on their lack of participation and their apathetic attitude.

On Christmas Eve of 1968 about fifty POWs at a prison we called the "Plantation" had unexpectedly been taken to a religious service. They were amazed and immediately began passing every shred of information they had back and forth. Three roommates were the "choir" at the front of the room. They also were heavily engaged in passing information. The sermon, by a V clergyman, likened Jesus to Ho Chi Minh and Herod to President Lyndon Johnson. The V filmed the entire show for propaganda.

The two guys next door to us in the Office had been two of those roommates and had sung in the "choir" for the Christmas Eve service of 1968. In the spring of 1970 the V took them to quiz and asked them if they wanted to put together a choir. They could practice and then entertain the rest of the POWs at a promised Christmas service. For the next several months, a few men from each of the various buildings in the Zoo were brought together in a room for choir practice. With so many prisoners face to face with each other for the first time, the choir became a beehive of communications activity. The guards tried halfheartedly and in vain to stop the exchange of information. Eventually they gave up. Whether or not a Christmas service ever came to pass, the opportunity to pass information so easily was wonderful.

During the dry season, the rope for the bucket broke and it was necessary to lower someone into the well to retrieve the bucket and tie it back onto the rope. John either volunteered or was drafted. As we were lowering him into the well, the rope broke again and John plummeted about fifteen feet. Fortunately, he did not land on the bucket, but in the two feet of mud at the bottom, straddling the bucket. Eventually we were able to double the rope and retrieve both John and the bucket.

That evening we bumped the entire building up on the back wall. With the attendant fanfare, lecture about the lack of participation in camp activities, and expression of disappointment from the recreation committee, we announced: the winner of the diving contest.

Some time later, the two guys next door reported to us that one of them, Norm, who did not know how to swim, was now taking swimming lessons. They had decided that Norm could learn to swim by lying on a small bench they had in the room and practicing his strokes. Every day or so we would get a progress report on Norm's swimming lessons.

In the monsoon season, it rained so much that the water level in the cistern would actually be above the level of the ground. After being out for their turn in the wash area, the two guys next door tapped to us, "Norm got into the well to practice his swimming in real water. He is progressing quite well. Treading water very easily for prolonged periods of time. It is difficult to accurately assess his crawl, breast or back strokes, because the diameter of the well is only three feet. So Norm can't really get horizontal enough in the water to demonstrate the full range of his prowess. However, the little he was able to do looked very good."

We were elated for Norm and the progress he was making. We did however, harbor a suspicion that beneath the murky well water, Norm may have had his feet pressed against the sides of the well.

We had begun re-remembering and memorizing everything. It was important to us, for some reason, to be able to recall the names of every teacher we had ever had, in chronological order; or to recall the name of the students in our fifth grade homerooms. It was amazing what we were able to remember.

The parents of another Norm — not the swimmer — had insisted when he was a child that every year he memorize a poem, which he would then have to recite at the annual family Thanksgiving dinner. He hated it, of course! But years later, sitting around in prison, Norm was able to recall great quantities of poetry.

A message would come tapping through the walls saying, "Norm is working on 'The Highwayman.' He is stuck on the line that comes after 'plaiting a dark red love knot into her long black hair.' Can anyone help?"

We loved to get those messages. For starters, we could discuss for days whether anyone had ever read "The Highwayman," heard of "The Highwayman," or knew anything about "The Highwayman." Then we could take more days to make up lots of lines and send them back to Norm. It didn't matter if anybody knew anything about

"The Highwayman." Norm was working hard over there, and we wanted to help.

Eventually, through the wall, a line at a time, would come "The Highwayman." And we would memorize it as it came. We had huge quantities of material memorized. Some of this we memorized for the sheer beauty of the words, like Robert Frost's poem, "Stopping by Woods on a Snowy Evening":

> Whose woods these are, I think I know
> His house is in the village though.
> He will not see me stopping here
> To watch his woods fill up with snow.
>
> My little horse must think it queer,
> To stop without a farm house near,
> Between the woods and frozen lake
> The darkest evening of the year.
>
> He gives his harness bells a shake
> To ask if there is some mistake.
> The only other sound's the sweep
> Of easy wind and downy flake.
>
> The woods are lovely, dark and deep,
> But I have promises to keep,
> And miles to go before I sleep,
> And miles to go before I sleep.

Some we memorized just for the sound of the words:

> There are strange things done in the midnight sun,
> by the men who moil for gold.
> And the arctic trails have their secret tales,
> that would make your blood run cold.

The Northern Lights have seen queer sights,
but the queerest they ever did see,
was the night on the marge of Lake Le Barge
where I cremated Sam McGee.
                    (from "The Cremation of Sam McGee,"
                                by Robert Service)

And some of the things that we memorized had a great deal of significance for us personally as we sat in those prisons:

If you can force your heart, and nerve and sinew
to serve their term long after they are gone.
And so go on when there is nothing in you
except the will that says to them hang on.
                    (from "If," by Rudyard Kipling)

In the fell clutch of circumstance,
I have not whined or cried aloud.
Under the bludgeoning of chance,
my head is bloody but unbowed.
                    (from "Invictus," by W. E. Henley)

Yea, though I walk through
the valley of the shadow of death,
I shall fear no evil, for thou art with me.
Thy rod and thy staff, they comfort me.
Thou preparest a table before me
in the presence of mine enemies.
Thou anointest my head with oil.
My cup runneth over.

                                (from Psalm 23)

It was natural, since we were so enamored with those poems, that we would try to write some ourselves. I wrote several poems for Karen, my fiancée and wife to be. This is one:

The night that we met, it rained, I recall
The Hi-Life, the movie, the oranges and all.

The places we'd been, the things we had seen
Paled in the mist round a yellow-clad dream.

Through the next few months, our love, how it grew
My world was aglow with, my darling, you.

Now times of duress and trouble and pain
My comfort comes from our love's sweet refrain.

You're strength when I'm weak, and joy when I'm sad
Courage 'gainst heartaches and problems I've had.

Your memory's with me, alone and afraid
Companion and refuge, never to fade.

Your love and your faith my guardian theme
Hope for the future, my yellow-clad dream.

I had that and two others written down and framed. I gave them to her the night before our wedding, six weeks after my release and return to the United States.

I remember the day a good friend of mine wrote his first poem. It was after the first meal of the day. That day we had bread instead of rice. Jerry took a bite out of his bread, looked down, and started his first poem. It went like this:

Little weevil in my bread,
I think I just bit off your head!

It went downhill from there, but at least it got him started.

Poetry was a great diversion. Over the years, John Borling composed many poems without paper or pencil, committing each new line to memory. He would review them frequently to keep them firm in his memory. Eventually John had written so many poems that it would take him days to review them all. At that point we were living together with four other men, and we began to memorize John's poems to help out with the archiving problem.

8

Duped

In October of 1970, the six of us were moved into a room in the "Pig Sty," a smaller building next to the Office. The Pig Sty had only four or five rooms, housing about twenty men in all. Several days after our arrival, the turnkey opened the doors to all the rooms at the same time, and we were allowed out into the courtyard together for the first time ever. Inquiry around the Zoo via the communications network revealed that the same thing was going on in the other buildings. This represented a huge change in our treatment, but even bigger changes were coming.

In late October, to our utter amazement, the V began building basketball backboards on stanchions in our courtyard. We knew through the communications network that other buildings were receiving a Ping-Pong table, or a volleyball net and ball. All the senior ranking officers (SROs) for the Zoo immediately began sending messages discussing how we would conduct ourselves. Their decision was that since everyone seemed to be having their quality of life upgraded, we should all take advantage of it. We began playing basketball.

The V showed up one day with a guitar and gave it to us — a guitar! We were certain the war must be over and we would be going home soon. There were two fellows with us in the Pig Sty who knew a little about music, so they began working diligently to figure out how the guitar was played. Those who were interested began taking lessons from them as fast as they were able to come up with chords and tunes. We "hot-boxed" that guitar, passing it from one to another all day long. The only time it wasn't played was when we were sleeping.

The V continued taking several guys from each building to choir practice in preparation for what they kept saying would be a big Christmas service. That practice continued to be one of the main conduits for communications between the buildings. It sure beat tapping on walls.

One of our ongoing efforts over the years had been trying to have the V recognize and deal with our chain of command. We had always insisted that they talk with the SRO at any quiz or other opportunity. They had always ignored our requests. It was part of their insistence that we were war criminals and not POWs. Therefore, we were not entitled to have our military organization recognized.

This decision process was typical. Whoever was senior in a group, or in whatever groups had contact with each other, was charged with making the final decision. We were military, after all. That decision process applied on questions of any scale. If you were alone you made the decision, in accordance with whatever guidance you had received about the situation you found yourself in. If you had no previous guidance, then it was up to you to do the best you could. If you were in contact with others, and it was possible, the decision was referred to the SRO; if it was not possible to refer the decision, you made it in accordance with his previous guidance. With few exceptions, I think that the Vietnamese saw us as a tightly unified body. They must have marveled at our strength and unity. That was all we showed to them.

Among ourselves, however, we would discuss and argue to the maximum extent imaginable. Aside from needing to choose between options, we were interested in passing the time. The SROs were always open to input and discussion — they wanted to pass the time too. In the final analysis, however, whoever was senior in a given situation made and was held responsible for all decisions.

The month of November passed by quite agreeably. Dick Ratzlaff and I decided to let our hair grow. We had received a few pictures from home, and it was obvious to us that men's hairstyles were getting longer. In prison the turnkey gave us hand shears — something like sheep shears — so we could cut our hair every few months.

After Dick and I had let our hair grow for several months, the V took our SRO out to a quiz. He was told that Dick and I must cut our hair. He relayed that when he returned. We were all amazed that the V were now dealing with the SRO; we had insisted on this the whole time we were there, and until now the V had ignored that request.

Although we were delighted that the V were dealing with the SRO, we were divided over how we should respond. Some thought we should comply. Dick and I, and some others, thought we should not comply until we saw how far they might be willing to push the issue. A huge discussion ensued. Finally, our SRO and his senior advisors decided that we should cut our hair.

Dick and I were led to the wash area by the turnkey, who gave us the shears. The two of us really did feel that we shouldn't do this without more pressure from the V. However, while we were cutting each other's hair, it dawned on us that no one had said how short to cut it. So we proceeded to cut it all off. That didn't meet with much approval from the rest of the roommates. The V looked pretty miffed, but said nothing.

It was astonishing that we were being left alone and were playing basketball every day. The V had even come around with a bag of canvas high-top shoes and given them to us for the basketball games. While we were playing one day in early December, around the corner of the Pig Sty came a group of about thirty photographers. Immediately, we sat down. The V were not happy. We were locked back up, and our SRO went to quiz.

The V insisted that we continue playing and that the photographers be allowed to take pictures. Our SRO refused, saying we would not provide such blatant propaganda. He was returned to the Pig Sty to think about it. Meanwhile, we had been in contact with the other buildings in the Zoo. The SROs were all "talking" through the communications network. At length, the decision was made that we would continue these activities and not be concerned about photographers. True was true, after all, and the quality of life in every building had been upgraded.

Just before Christmas of 1970, numerous photographs were taken of us playing basketball and the guitar. The Christmas service did materialize, and pictures of all of this appeared in *Life* magazine.

9

Unity

Two days after Christmas, we were instructed to roll up our meager belongings, and we were all moved. Every building in the Zoo and Annex was emptied. Although we had no way of knowing it, the same thing was happening in all the POW prisons in and around Hanoi. Although we wouldn't know why for a long time, there was a reason.

On November 2, 1970, the United States had raided a POW prison called Son Tay, about 30 kilometers west of Hanoi. The raid came in one night like the wrath of God — a team of seventy U.S. Army Special Forces troops, in helicopters augmented by gun ships. They landed in the middle of Son Tay to rescue American POWs. Unfortunately, intelligence was a little behind: four months before the raid, the North Vietnamese had moved all Americans out of Son Tay. This raid resulted in a consolidation of POWs from the smaller prison camps into the larger prisons of Hanoi early in December. This consolidation looked like merely another move in the lives of the POWs involved. Since we had no communications between prisons, we were unaware that all the smaller prisons had been closed.

We didn't know anything about the Son Tay raid for many months, but through December we noticed that the Vietnamese guards seemed very nervous. The number of guards was increased. All our captors seemed more uptight. Within days after the Christmas picture-taking session, they had moved all American POWs from all the prisons around Hanoi into the back of Hua Lo, the big prison downtown.

The back section of Hua Lo was a huge, roughly rectangular complex about 100 yards long, with large cells all around the perimeter. The Vietnamese put thirty to fifty Americans into each cell, usually with an empty cell or two in between. It was wonderful; we had never been in such large groups, nor had all of us ever been in the same place at the same time.

The twenty of us from the Pig Sty found ourselves in a cell in the middle of one of the shorter legs of the rectangle. The cell adjoining ours on our left was empty. To the left of the empty cell there was a complex of smaller cells, into which the V had moved the senior ranking American officers, thirty-three in all.

To our right (again facing the center of the rectangle), there was a cell in which the Vietnamese placed three Cambodian prisoners and a captured South Vietnamese pilot. To the right of that cell, they moved seven Americans who, up to that time, had very little contact with the rest of us. Then on our far right, beyond them, there was a driveway that gave access to the interior of the rectangle.

In our cell there was a foot-wide ledge along the back wall, eighteen inches from the ceiling. At each end of the ledge was a small barred window. Outside, behind our cell, was a narrow alley, and beyond that the back wall of the prison. We communicated with the senior officers through the nearest room of men on our left. We would lie on the ledge and cough a couple of times out the window. They would cough back. Those initial coughs meant we were all looking for guards near our cells or in the alley. After an hour or so, if we saw no guards, we would cough again. They would do the same if they had not seen or heard any guards in the alley. Then, knowing it was all clear, we could talk softly back and forth in the alley, and they would relay it to the senior officers.

From their cell, the senior officers were able to flash to the large cell on the leg of the rectangle nearest to them. Then, via tap code or flashing, the cells were able to communicate all the way around the courtyard. The only exception was that no one had contact with the seven at the other end of our cell block, two rooms to our right.

It was an exciting time for all of us. We were all together in the same place at the same time and nearly everyone was in contact. We got organized! We became the Fourth Allied POW Wing, named in succession after the previous three major conflicts in which Americans and their allies were imprisoned together: World War I, World War II, and the Korean conflict. We named this big prison in the back of Hua Lo "Unity."

The senior officers codified all the bits and pieces of guidance that had been initiated and passed around for years. One day as we were talking down the alley, the senior officers told us they were going to make official the instructions by which we were to live and govern ourselves while we were in prison. Everyone was to memorize the instructions, which were to be called "plums." (Everything in the military has to have a code name.) Over the next several weeks we received all the plums; and so did everyone else, except the isolated seven. It was wonderful that we were all getting the same rules at the same time, officially.

The Fourth Allied POW Wing Policies (Plums) were as follows:

1. Wing Policy # 1 — Command Authority

Any POW who denies or fails to carry out the Code of Conduct, Military Law or Wing Policies may be relieved of all military authority. Emotional instability so serious as to impair judgment for a prolonged period of time may be cause for relief. Only the Wing Commanding Officer (WCO), the Acting Wing Commanding Officer (AWCO) or the Senior Ranking Officer (SRO) for geographically detached units had the authority to relieve or reinstate. This action was to be based on current performance, not the past, nor hearsay. It is neither American nor Christian to nag a repentant sinner to the grave.

2. Wing Policy # 2 — Objectives
Part I Background

The considerable improvements we have noted have been due primarily to external sources and to nothing we have done ourselves. We do not want to take a step backwards but we do want to oppose those things that are wrong. Be firm but reasonable.

Part II Things that are wrong
A. Inhumane treatment such as stocks, isolation, etc.
B. Insufficient opportunity to air legitimate grievances to the camp authorities.
C. Interference with our letters and packages.

Part III Things we want
A. POW status.
B. Senior Ranking Officers to meet with camp authorities to help administer the camp.

C. More outside time; sports such as volleyball.

D. Educational materials.

E. More and better food.

Part IV How to get the things we want

A. Do not react to petty annoyances.

B. Firmly oppose those things that are wrong.

C. Work with camp authorities for improved welfare of all.

3. Wing Policy # 3 — POW Conduct

A. Main points of the Code of Conduct:

1. Do not condemn, deny, or say anything detrimental about the United States, or its allies or their cause.

2. Do not accept special favors, including parole.

B. Resistance and Tactics:

1. Take torture to resist the following: written propaganda; making tapes; bowing; making public appearances; writing or signing anything involving crimes or trials including pleas; giving military information; giving Wing secrets such as organization, internal communication, etc.

2. The objective is to give the enemy nothing. In any case minimize the enemy net gain by the use of moral courage, physical strength, trickery, and cover stories involving only oneself and pre-briefed cohorts.

3. It may be prudent to limit the taking of physical torture to the point short of the loss of mental skills. However, this point should not be short of significant pain nor reached solely through self-induced punishment such as sitting on stool, kneeling, etc.

4. If you take hard knocks, roll with the punches and bounce back to win the next round.

C. No writing statements except as follows:

1. For urgent reasons of health.

2. To minimize the net gain to the enemy. A POW who writes a statement for either reason above must justify his actions as soon as possible to the WCO in a Conduct Exception Report (CER). Senior ranking officers may write piecemeal administrative info providing it benefits the Wing and an oral presentation is not feasible. In any case writing under the above exceptions must not give the enemy propaganda.

D. Equal treatment:

1. Accept and use improvement items within the Reasonable Time Frame (RTF) set by the WCO.

2. Turn in items that have not spread to the majority during the RTF.

3. Nullify the enemy attempts to use improvement items for propaganda by turning them in if necessary.

4. Wing Policy # 4 — Resistance Conditions (RESCONS)

This is a planned disobedience of the North Vietnamese (V) restriction against making noise. It is to be used to protest grievous wrongs. Past experience has shown that the V may react with anti-riot action and extreme caution should be used in its execution.

RESCON One — Sing

A. Sing the national anthem. This will be initiated by a message from the WCO or by the WCO's living group singing the "Notre Dame Fight Song."

B. Sing "The Star-Spangled Banner" and songs of your choice repeating "The Star Spangled Banner" for two days or until the SRO expects the threat of anti-riot action. This will be initiated by message or by singing "Roll Out the Barrel" from the WCO living group.

RESCON Two — Squat

This is a planned diet for one to two weeks. Turn back one-half your food in a manner that is clearly visible to the V and ensure they know why you are doing it. The sick and wounded are excluded from the diet. Go outside only for medical treatment, interrogations, or an SRO assigned task.

RESCON Three — Soldier

Conduct all outside activities in military formations. Give the impression of threats to higher escalation. Use variety and imagination in its execution.

RESCON Four — Stir

Lessen your cooperation with the V and ensure they know why you are doing it. Maintain strict order and discipline in this and all other escalations. Avoid direct confrontations with the V that would result in the man being removed from the room.

RESCON Five — Stance (our normal RESCON)

Conduct yourselves as officers and gentlemen. Maintain strict order and discipline. Avoid self-degradation and exploitation. Show composure and reserved civility toward the V. Maintain a low-order risk, erosive type resistance.

Remarks: Only the WCO or Deputy WCO can authorize RESCON One. SROs may escalate to four and return to one without prior permission. RESCONS are not cumulative.

5. Wing Policy # 5 — Release
Objective — Honorable release for all. Honorable release may be all together or incremental or through a legitimate third party or expulsion. Prefer sick and wounded first; enlisted; civilians; and officers in order of capture. WCO and Deputy WCO will go last. Only WCO can approve release. No POW can negotiate own release. If at any time during the release sequence it becomes evident that the release would meet with US Government disapproval, the release will be refused and resisted. Foresee three situations likely:

Situation One: Vietnamese continue early release of few for propaganda. This violates Code of Conduct. Action: Refuse and resist.

Situation Two: Vietnamese withhold details or refuse to allow WCO approval. Action: Force Vietnamese to expel you.
A. Make strong effort to see WCO.
B. State "I want to go home in my turn after the sick and wounded without fancy clothes and the Code of Conduct requires me to resist propaganda." Caution: Be firm or the Vietnamese may mark you for propaganda.
C. Thereafter, go in silence. Do not write, sign, or say anything except as approved by U.S. government

representative. Do nothing to hamper honorable release of others. OK to sign for personal effects.

D. Resist association with known civilian propaganda groups or participation in propaganda activities. Normal candid news photography is not propaganda. Work through your senior officer in accordance with Wing Policy #1.

Situation Three: Vietnamese publicize formal agreement between governments. Action: Same as Situation Two except SRO in communication or SRO of Detachment can take any common sense action within the Code of Conduct to effect a smooth release.

6. Wing Policy #6 — Post Release Behavior Standards

A. Our attitude at time of release should reflect our pride in our country during this most difficult period.

B. A man's most prized possession is his reputation. Do not make any derogatory remarks concerning the behavior of other POWs except before an official inquiry and then stick to the facts.

C. This principle of military and Christian behavior applies here while we are still POWs.

7. Wing Policy # 7 — Open Door Policy

A. Any POW may submit to the WCO or detachment SRO through normal communications channels:

1. Request for redress of grievances.

2. Request for relief from any Wing Policy or portion thereof for personal reasons.

3. Suggestions and Recommendations. These may be endorsed as appropriate up through channels. Flag link available if matter is personal.

If communications is cut, the senior SRO in communications will assume command and report the action taken when communications is restored.

In addition to these formal regulations, we followed a policy expressed in the acronym "BACK US," which meant:

B. Bowing — Do not bow in public, that is, under camera surveillance of non-prison authorities.

A. Air — Stay off the air. Stay off the radios. Stay off the tapes.

C. Crimes — Admit no crimes. Avoid using the Vietnamese word for "violation." (Stockdale realized this could not be resisted entirely, but the word "crime" should be avoided if at all possible.)

K. Kiss — Do not kiss the Vietnamese goodbye. (This was aimed directly at a future release program, in which he believed that the Vietnamese would require the prisoners to say "Thank you for your generosity." This he felt would be beneath the prisoners' dignity.)

U. Unity

S. Self — The U & S in combination form "Unity over Self."

Later the senior officers announced that we would have a mission statement. As with the plums, everyone memorized the mission statement, and it guided all our activity. Our mission was "Return with Honor." We all knew the mission, and every day we were trying to accomplish it. The mission statement was intended to give everyone an understanding of what we were trying to achieve, and to make sure we were all pulling on our oars in the same direction.

Individuals in a group function, for the most part, based on their understanding of what it means to be part of that organization. People develop a mental model of what a person who works in this organization does, how he behaves, what he is oriented toward. No one really works out of three-ring binders full of guidelines and instructions — most of which are written so that people can be prosecuted after the fact if they make mistakes or fail to read senior managers' minds. A mission statement is an attempt to keep everyone's mental model aligned in the same direction. However, this presupposes that everyone knows what the mission statement is.

It helped greatly that we had a common mission. "Return with Honor" was our reason to get up every morning, an opportunity to see each day as a chance to excel. It would have been pretty hard to get excited about just surviving and getting through the day. But now we had a mission statement that would stimulate and excite us, demand our best, and put us clearly beyond mere survival. We had a mission, we knew the mission, we tried to live the mission; daily, we breathed the mission.

In order to achieve that level of commitment, we all had to be involved. Involvement is the key to commitment. In the prisons of Hanoi, we were all involved in everything that happened. We gave input, solicited or unsolicited. We argued and debated. I cannot remember one time when our senior leadership was closed to input, discussion, or even debate. We were all involved; therefore, we were committed.

Since the group who were relaying between us and the senior officers had been shot down relatively recently, we began to pump them for news from the United States. In our room we had numerous "old hands," guys who had been

prisoners for years before I arrived. Each day we would give
the relay group a topic, such as "Tell us about the new auto-
mobiles in the U.S." They would talk it over among themselves, and the next day they would give us as much of an
update as possible on that subject.

Along with infrequent letters, some of us had received
a few photographs from home. One picture I had was
troubling me: it was my brother Dan at his college graduation — with long hair. When we had left the U.S. in the
early to mid-1960s, the only men who had long hair were
hippie dope smokers from the Haight-Ashbury in San
Francisco. Needless to say, that group was not very much
appreciated by us sitting in prison in North Vietnam.

Dan's long hair was troubling to us, and particularly to
me. We had a running discussion about whether my brother
was a hippie. We wanted to ask the relay group about men
with long hair, but without predisposing their answer.
Rather than ask just about men's hairstyles, we decided to
ask about men's fashions in general.

That evening we asked them to give us a report on
men's clothes, shoes, and hairstyles. They had a long,
heated discussion among themselves (we later learned)
about how to handle that question. Men's styles were
changing rapidly: long hair was very much in vogue,
polyester was coming into style, and men's clothes could be
flashy enough to make your eyes cross.

One of the men in our room was Ev Alvarez, the first
American POW, who had been shot down in 1964. Others
had been there since 1965 and 1966. The new relay group
decided that the truth might be too upsetting for us. So that
night, after we finished our business, we said, "OK, tell us
about men's fashions." They replied, "There really haven't
been very many changes at all."

I sat there looking at the picture of my brother with his
long hair. I was crushed. I had a weirdo, long-haired hippie

freak for a brother. Later we learned that most men in the U.S. were wearing their hair longer, but it was a sad couple of years until I found that out.

On an irregular schedule — probably about every eight to twelve months — we were moved from prison to prison and from cell to cell. Living with different people gave us new opportunities to enrich our impoverished existence by learning from one another. It was stimulating to be moved in with someone who could teach you something — anything.

We chose to make a determined effort to learn and grow. We were not going to sit around in those prisons and vegetate; we were going to come out of there better than we were when we got shot down. We began to teach each other everything we had ever learned — and a number of things we had never learned!

I learned to play the piano in prison, from a fellow who had taken piano lessons as a child. One day we decided that I should learn, so we took toilet paper and glued it together with rice. We took ashes and dirt and drew a keyboard on it. John then taught me how to read the keyboard and how to read music, and all the little finger exercises that piano students use.

I practiced faithfully. On Sundays, I would give concerts, spreading out my piano at the end of the cell. I have played some of the most beautiful music in the world, with great enthusiasm. My cellmates loved it, of course. Well, if they didn't like what I was playing, they could listen to something else. They would applaud wildly and ask for more. I always tried to leave them begging.

Since I have been home, I have occasionally seated myself in front of a real piano. I don't know what was wrong with that piano. The music wasn't anything like it had been in my head. It was — to be brutally honest —

terrible. It had been perfectly beautiful in my head, but whenever I attempt to play a real piano, it's awful.

Actually, I find many things are like that: perfect in my head. Maybe you're that way, too. How about the way you plan to get organized? Or the communications process? It's perfect in my head: what I want to say, what needs to be done, the reasoning behind it. But then I have to get it out of there and over to someone else. It always ends up much less perfect.

I learned to type in prison, too, by the same sort of process. A fellow POW who knew how to type taught me the keyboard — ASDFG, etc. I folded my blanket into a slanted shape, pulled a white thread out of the border, and sewed it onto the slanted portion in big stitches. There was a stitch where each typewriter key should be. Then I practiced for days. I typed my memoirs several times: they kept getting better. I typed letters to everyone I knew. When I was typing on my blanket I never had to use the backspace key; I didn't make any mistakes.

It would be enough for someone to mention, for instance, that he had taken a geology course. We would immediately make him the "geology professor." The process was the same as we used for movies. He would find out what his cellmates knew about rocks, mud, dirt, and so on, then tap a message on the walls and inquire around the prison. Eventually he knew everything anyone knew about geology. At that point he began to teach the geology course.

I had studied a lot of mathematics at the Naval Academy. I did pretty well, but I never really understood how it all worked together until I lived for months with Charlie Zuhoski, whom we called "the Wizard." The Wizard had managed to cram four years of a mathematics major at Rensselaer Polytechnical Institute into five and a half years. Using a piece of brick to write on the floor of our cell, the Wizard taught me advanced math — and I understood it!

At one time we had a speech class. We were a group of men who were locked up, twenty-four hours a day, seven days a week, three hundred and sixty-five days a year. Our language deteriorated so badly that we could not speak without using four-letter words. We used them for everything: capitalization, hyphenation, exclamation, declaration!

But one day it dawned on us that it would be unacceptable for us to talk that way when we got back to the United States. The more energetic among us decided that every time we slipped and said a four-letter word, we would do five push-ups. Well, by about seven o'clock in the morning, my arms would be aching from doing push-ups!

We then decided we needed to do something to train ourselves to speak more acceptably. We discovered that John, my piano teacher, had been active in the Forensic Society at the Air Force Academy. He knew all about speeches and speaking. Another cellmate had been in Toastmasters. So we started the Hanoi chapter of Toastmasters and held very formal speech classes for five or six hours, one day a week.

One person was assigned to be the master of ceremonies. Someone else would be assigned to prepare a twenty-minute sales presentation on the electrical manufacturing application of left-handed widgets, for example. Another person had to prepare a fifteen-minute informative presentation on, say, the mating habits of bull elephants. There were impromptu and extemporaneous speeches. We had judges. We had an "ah" counter to enumerate all the mental hiccups — "ah," "like," "you know." In the back of the room, some poor soul was the timekeeper. He had to count the seconds to himself: one thousand one, one thousand two, one thousand three. Then he would hold up his fingers so we could see how much time had gone by on the "clock."

The speech class went so well that we decided to have a college-style debate. We paired off into teams and developed the statement to be debated for the season. On debate day, once a week, the first "pro" speaker would lead off, followed by the first "con." Then there would be the first rebuttal, followed by the second rebuttal.

Debating was great fun, mainly because we did not have any resource material, so we just made it all up. It became an exercise in creative thinking. Your opponent would say something like, "I cite the article in *Newsweek* from July of 1970 in which the distinguished Dr. Jones from the University of Alabama cited the results of his research which conclusively proved...."

When your turn for rebuttal came, you could point out that while your opponent correctly quoted Dr. Jones, he had overlooked the articles more recently published in the *New England Journal of Medicine,* September of 1970, which directly contradicted the findings from the University of Alabama.

When I was with the group of twenty men, it turned out that only about six of them were married. We came up with the idea that the married roommates should provide the bachelors with a marriage counseling class. We argued that someday, should we get married, there was no need for us to make all the same mistakes they had already made.

The married gurus loved it. They would confer for hours and hours during the week, and on the appointed day the class would convene. The gurus would seat themselves as a panel at one end of the cell, and we, the students, would sit at their feet.

They taught us everything there is to know about women, from female anatomy to what makes them tick. After I had been married for a while, it became very clear to me why they had some of the problems they had in their marriages. They had some pretty interesting ideas about marriage and women.

We ran an Officer Candidate School (OCS). There were three Air Force enlisted airmen with us who had been the crew on an Air Force Jolly Green rescue helicopter that had been shot down. One day we got to thinking that these three guys were going through the same experience we were, and they were doing a very good job of it. Maybe we should give them battlefield commissions.

We had no idea how to do that, but that did not slow us down. We proposed the idea of battlefield commissions by tapping it through the walls to the senior officer in the prison where we were at the time. He agreed to it, and so we instituted our OCS.

The three enlisted men had to sit and listen to anything and everything the other seventeen of us could think of that had anything to do with military strategy, military history, or anything else even remotely related to the military. After weeks of suffering through our rambling discourses, they raised their right hands, and we administered the oath and commissioned them as second lieutenants in the United States Air Force.

Upon our return to the United States, we informed the Air Force of what we had done. Not only that: we argued that the three had now been alive long enough so that they were no longer second lieutenants; they would have been promoted to first lieutenants. (Usually living long enough as a second lieutenant is the primary prerequisite for promotion to first lieutenant. The other prerequisite is whether a fog forms on a mirror that is held under your nose as proof that you are still breathing!) Not knowing what to do, and not wanting to upset us, the Air Force went along with the battlefield commissions, backdating their date of rank to the original commissioning date and promoting the three to first lieutenant.

We taught each other many things. I learned how to play cards when I was in prison. We made the cards out of toilet paper. We learned every card game imaginable. When we played bridge, we would simultaneously use every convention there is. If you play bridge for hours and hours on end, day after day, you can do that. I can tell you one thing about toilet paper cards: they were doggone hard to shuffle.

We also drew a craps table on the floor and ground a couple pieces of brick into square dice. Then we all learned to play craps. After learning our way around a craps table pretty well we began to wonder how much money was really necessary to play craps right. How much should someone have so that he could weather the down side until his luck turned and he started winning? It was the perfect challenge for the Wizard, our resident mathematician.

We decided to use Mom's craps table as the basis for our calculations. Mom's was a little casino in Fallon, Nevada, where the Navy had an airfield. When an air wing was preparing to be deployed aboard a carrier, part of the training cycle included two weeks of training at Fallon, where they could practice bombing, tactics, and air combat maneuvering without disturbing anyone except the ground squirrels. Those training periods always included numerous trips to Mom's, trying to win our fortunes.

The appeal of Mom's, aside from the fact that she loved naval aviators and was old enough to be our mother, was that Mom had a craps table where the minimum bet was a dime. Using Mom's dime craps table as a model, the

Wizard figured out that someone would need at least three thousand dollars to eventually win. That was pretty sobering.

How creative does all of this sound? Very creative! However, prior to being shot down, I didn't think of myself as creative. Me, creative? I'd been in the Navy since high school. You don't get real creative flying high-performance military airplanes. Yet I found myself with all these men, and we had tremendous creativity within us.

I'm now convinced that every person is potentially very creative. Typically, the limits on our creativity are self-imposed. We do not allow or encourage ourselves to be innovative, but my experience taught me that this is possible for all of us.

There are three factors that I think are important if you want to be creative. First, it takes time. In the helter-skelter rush of daily life, you don't have time to explore possibilities. Second, it has to be safe, or at least relatively risk-free; we have to have a relatively safe environment to explore "what ifs." And third, it takes motivation — a need or a reason to want to be creative. There must be some force pushing us in that direction, some reason we would want to explore different potentials. In Hanoi we had all three factors working for us.

10

We Had Our Problems

Off and on over the years, we had some difficulties with one another. Being locked up under such close circumstances tried even the most patient among us on occasion. Fortunately, we had, at least to my knowledge, very few serious problems, though minor problems were not all that uncommon.

The minor difficulties generally centered around differences of opinion, disagreements, and personality clashes. In such a close, forced living situation, under a lot of stress, nerves would get frayed, and molehills sometimes became mountains. I think one of the biggest lessons we learned was to deal with problems and disagreements when they happened, and not to delay or pretend things were all right.

The real problem with all the minor annoyances was that at the end of the day, we weren't going home. We had no idea if we would ever get a break from each other. Any minor conflict was probably just going to fester and grow if we didn't try to deal with it and resolve it.

The only way we had to work on problems was through talking. For the most part, then, it became common

practice to start talking immediately and try to deal with
disagreements and differences. Many times we also had
mediators, whether we wanted them or not! After all, life
was pretty boring, and other cellmates were not about to
miss an opportunity to be involved — perhaps even help —
with any little tiffs. I am unable to remember any really
long-standing difficulties that we had among ourselves,
though I'm sure there were some. We had individuals who
just could not get along with each other, but fortunately,
they rarely had to live together.

Nonetheless, we had one very serious problem. I am
going to relate my version of the story here. I know there
may be other versions, but this is what I remember about it.
This problem involved two individuals who were actively
involved in aiding, abetting and collaborating with the
enemy. We were not aware of this for several years.

There was a Marine Corps aviator, an F-4 squadron
commanding officer, who was shot down. I'll call him "the
Colonel." I think the Colonel was the only totally amoral
person I've ever known. As soon as he was shot down and
captured, he recognized immediately that the game had
changed and decided to cooperate with his captors.

The V kept him quite isolated. The rest of us had
little if any contact with him; in fact, for a long time most
of us didn't even know he existed. Much later, after talking
with him for hours, I became convinced that he rational-
ized his behavior in order to make his life there more
comfortable.

The other person in this episode was a naval aviator,
also an F-4 squadron commanding officer. I'll call him "the
Commander." He was shot down while on a vector for a
MIG. The radar ship off shore was giving him directions,
telling him which way to turn, with the objective of having
him arrive behind the MIG in a firing position.

Unfortunately, either the controller turned the Commander too tightly, or he pulled his aircraft too hard in the turn. Instead of rolling out of his turn behind the MIG in a firing position, the Commander flew out in front of the MIG, and since the belly of his aircraft was toward the MIG as he was turning, he never saw it. The MIG fired a missile and shot the Commander down. The Radar Intercept Officer (RIO) in the back seat of his airplane was killed by the missile.

The Commander ejected and was immediately captured, thrown in a truck, and taken to Hanoi. When he stepped out of the truck in Hanoi, he had a stroke that paralyzed one side of his body. The Vietnamese threw him in an isolated cell and, over time, he largely recovered from the stroke.

During his recovery period, the interrogators used to go into his cell and practice their English with him. They also gave him a lot of Hanoi-published material to read. Their magazines and books contained a high proportion of sheer propaganda. For example, in a volume of Vietnamese studies dealing with the end of World War II, it says, "The war in the Pacific theater came to an end as a result of the crushing blows being dealt to the imperialistic, warmongering Japanese Army in South East Asia by the Peoples Liberation forces of North Vietnam." They invented history to suit their purpose.

I believe the Commander experienced something close to brainwashing because of his weakened condition and intensive exposure to propaganda. He internalized false and twisted information and logic. In the final analysis, I think he did it to himself.

I suppose there were two reasons for this. One was that the Commander was carrying a terrible load of guilt for the death of his RIO. Those two had flown together as a crew for nearly two years and had formed a very close professional and personal relationship.

I believe the second reason he brainwashed himself was that deep down, the Commander knew that if the V beat or tortured him, he would die. His damaged body would not have been strong enough to withstand further punishment. (I'm also certain that he would disagree with my analysis. I don't think he would have seen himself the way I've described him. He would have many other explanations and reasons for his conduct.)

Eventually the V put these two fellows together. The rest of us still didn't know they existed. The next step was a decision by the Vietnamese to put some other Americans in with these two to see what would happen. I can just picture the Vietnamese officers sitting around their headquarters one day and one of them saying, "I wonder what would happen if we took the next American we captured and, instead of working him over and putting him in with all the others who are constantly resisting, we put him in with the Colonel and the Commander?" Over the course of the next year and a half or so, they put five other Americans — whom they had not beaten — in with these two.

About two-thirds of the time I was a POW, there would be a radio speaker in the cell. It looked like it had been ripped out of the back of a car. It was hung by wires through the air vents high in the walls of most cells and wired directly into the prison headquarters. Over these speakers the V would, on occasion, play the Voice of Vietnam in English, a woman announcer whom we knew as "Hanoi Hannah"; or antiwar speeches and protests from the U.S. or from visiting delegations, like Jane Fonda, Ramsey Clark, or eastern Europeans. Sometimes they played confessions and other statements they had tortured out of one of our fellow POWs.

One day the prison officer came on the radio speaker. He said that they were going to play for us a tape of several of our comrades discussing the illegal, immoral war in

Vietnam. This tape was our first clue of the situation with the Colonel and the Commander. It was a recording of two Americans discussing the illegality and immorality of the war. They were saying that international law probably didn't apply here; that neither the Code of Conduct, nor the Geneva Conventions, nor the Uniform Code of Military Justice were applicable; that we were most likely war criminals, not POWs; they went on and on.

Our first reaction was to recoil and say, "Who can that be? Somebody's been tortured terribly. They must have had the crap beaten out of them to make them say those things." However, the longer we listened, the more we realized that, first of all, there was no stress in their voices. When we were beaten or tortured to make us say things we didn't want to say there would be tremendous stress in our voices, and we were experts at recognizing it.

Second, in a country where English was a foreign language, we native English speakers could do all sorts of things with our language that other English speakers would immediately recognize as strange. For example, we could emphasize the wrong syllable of a word, or use words that were archaic or not very appropriate. Those nuances were something that our captors never were able to recognize. The tape we were listening to had nothing like this. In fact, it sounded as if these guys were sitting down in a coffee shop, chatting about the war.

The walls came alive with tapping. "Who was that? Has anyone been forced to say things like that? Who could that have been?" It was our first clue that something was going on about which we knew nothing, absolutely nothing. And it wasn't anything good.

One day at the prison we called "Unity," when we were up on the ledge whispering down the alley with the relay group, they said, "We have information from around the rectangle. There is an empty cell on the other side of

you, and then there is a cell which has six or seven
Americans in it. No one knows who they are. We suspect
they may be the people who made the tape we heard months
ago — the tape which sounded like a discussion two people
were having and agreeing completely with the enemy.
Remember that tape? When no one knew who the speakers
were. Make contact with them as soon as possible."

Coincidentally, the V officers came in presently and
told us that we could play volleyball with the Americans in
another cell. It turned out to be that isolated cell. We were
anxious to make contact and planned to have one person
responsible for talking at length with each of them during
the game. Our whole objective was to find out who they
were and what they were up to.

Five of them were very receptive, but the Colonel and
the Commander were pretty cool toward us and rather than
talking, they insisted on playing volleyball. We conveyed a
lot of information to them and could see that most of it was
troubling to them. We played volleyball two different times,
and then never again.

The senior officers urged us to do whatever we had to
in order to maintain contact with the seven isolated
prisoners. First we tried to cough to them down the alley
behind the building. No response. The next day the senior
officers acknowledged that they heard the coughing: did we
make contact? We replied, "No, there was no response."
They urged us to continue trying.

After a couple of days with no results, the senior
officers said. "If there is as much as a fifty-fifty chance get
in touch with those guys." Back on the ledge, we coughed
louder and louder; eventually we gave up on the coughing
and began, quietly at first, to call down the alley.
Eventually we were shouting down the alley, trying to get
somebody to answer. All the while, we were cringing in the
knowledge that any moment, if the V heard us, the guards

would come bursting through the doors and the beatings would start.

Finally, after what seemed like an eternity, an answer came back down the alley. "Hey, are you Americans? Who are you? We need to talk. Are you the group we played volleyball with?" Finally we quieted them down and explained the coughing and clearing procedures to them.

After an hour, we coughed the clear signal and began to pass more and more information to them. They were happy to be in contact. No, they had not been treated roughly. Yes, two of them had made the tape we heard several months ago. It was merely a discussion about the war they were having. Indeed, they had civilian clothes, were being treated very well, and had been out in Hanoi several times to see delegations.

It immediately became clear that they were having a very different experience here in Hanoi than the rest of us. We told them to forget about watching for guards and to get everyone over near the window so they could all hear us. We then gave them a condensed version (it took about 45 minutes) of exactly what was going on in North Vietnam with American POWs. Every one of us had been repeatedly beaten and often tortured. International law did apply in this instance, as did the Geneva Conventions, the Code of Conduct, and the Uniform Code of Military Justice. Neither they nor we were war criminals, but in fact we all were prisoners of war. They were immediately to stop cooperating with the enemy.

By the end of the conversation, five of them were anxious to get back into the fold. We told them what the standard issue of clothing and equipment was and that they could keep those items and were to get rid of everything else — throw it out the door, if necessary. We gave them the plums and mission statement and told them to memorize them.

Almost instantaneously, five of them did an about-face. That left the Colonel and the Commander, who proceeded to tell us they disagreed with our position and didn't think the war was legal; based on that illegality, they thought the Uniform Code of Military Justice didn't apply in this situation; and they had many more objections.

We went to the other end of our ledge and reported to the senior officers. They were pleased and instructed us to keep working on the Colonel and the Commander. After several fruitless discussions with the two, which we faithfully relayed between them and the senior officers, the latter told us to give them a direct order to cease aiding and abetting the enemy.

All of these discussions could take hours. When we gave the Colonel and the Commander the direct order, they began a lengthy response. As they told it to us, we each memorized part of it. When we reestablished contact with the senior officers at the other end of the alley, each of us regurgitated his part of what the Colonel and the Commander had told us.

After hours and hours of discussions back and forth, the senior officers finally told us to relieve the Colonel and the Commander of all authority under the Uniform Code of Military Justice, which we promptly did. This meant that they would have no rank or authority. Naturally, the two of them didn't agree with this and had lengthy and repetitious rebuttals, which were relayed to the senior officers.

One day in our cell, we had a brilliant idea. We told the senior officers that given any opportunity in the future we would have a blanket party for the Colonel and the Commander, and we would square them away! (A blanket party is an exercise in which a group would throw a blanket over someone's head and beat him. It is not a subtle form of persuasion.) The senior officers' response was that we would never physically force them into compliance, but we were never to stop trying to convince them that they were wrong.

"Bummer," we thought, "we shouldn't have told them our idea." They were right, of course. It was not our prerogative to physically force compliance, nor ever to abandon any of our number, no matter the circumstances. We were in this together. And "Return with Honor" was the goal.

We remained in Camp Unity there for almost ten months, until October of 1971.

11

Back to the Zoo, and the Pig Sty Again

By October of 1971, the V were comfortable enough to move all of us back out to various prisons around Hanoi. The twenty from our cell were moved back into five rooms in the Pig Sty, a building in the Zoo. Four of the seven Americans with whom we had gotten in touch at Unity were added to our number. In the back of the Pig Sty, there was a small two-man room into which the Colonel and the Commander were moved. I don't recall that they were ever locked up. They would come around at all hours, open our shutters, lean on the bars, and talk with us. Our instructions were never to stop trying to get them on board.

This led to many lengthy discussions, not only about the war but also about life, flying, homes, families — everything. It was those discussions that led me to my conclusions that the Colonel was amoral and opportunistic, and that the Commander had brainwashed himself.

Following our return to the United States, we brought courts martial charges against the two of them. Admiral Stockdale, the senior naval officer among the POWs, pressed the charges. Eventually, however, the Secretary of the Navy made the decision to dismiss the charges and allow the Colonel and the Commander to retire quietly.

Jerry Coffee, another Navy pilot who had been part of our twenty-man group, and I sent a telegram to the Secretary of the Navy, telling him that we disagreed with his decision and thought he was making a grave mistake. This decision would set a terrible precedent for military personnel who might find themselves in POW situations in later conflicts. It was the only telegram I've ever sent to the Secretary of the Navy. He did not respond.

I'm sure that decision was politically motivated. The United States had been torn apart by the war in Vietnam. It was a raw nerve around which debate raged. Our country was desperately looking for something good to come out of that chapter of U.S. history — something honorable to which the nation could cling.

When we were finally released, it was a very high-profile event. The first ex-POW to step onto American soil after so many years in captivity was Admiral Jerry Denton. As he stepped from the airplane which carried him back to the United States, he made the following statement: "We are honored to have had the opportunity to serve our country under very difficult and trying circumstances. We are grateful to our nation and to President Nixon for bringing us home. God bless America."

He could have said anything, of course. He could have complained about being abandoned and rotting in prison for six years. But he stated exactly what we felt about what we had been through. That turned out to be something good — something truly exemplary, something healing around which the country could rally, acknowledge, and celebrate. We instantly became heroes.

The returning POWs immediately became bright and shining stars in what was otherwise a very painful and dingy chapter of our country's history. We came home to a hero's welcome. There was a political desire not to sully that shining image. There was hope to heal the nation to some extent through us. The disposition of the case of the Colonel and the Commander was part of that political effort.

Once we had been moved back to the Pig Sty, all the cells were unlocked at the same time on most days, and we were allowed out into the courtyard together to wash, empty buckets, and eat. The basketball stanchions were still there, reminding us how we had been duped into those pictures a year before. There was no basketball this time around.

In April of 1972, my piano teacher John, Mike Brazelton, and I were moved out of the Pig Sty and back into Unity, the big prison in the back of Hoa Loa. We ended up in one of the big rooms around the rectangle with forty-some other guys. It was a good move for us. We were with many men whose names and stories we knew, but whom we had never seen. I immediately had a new French class.

Later that month the U.S. bombing once again reached the Hanoi area, the first attack on targets in and near the city since March 1968. We were delighted that the war was coming back to Hanoi. We cheered as air raids shook our buildings. At the same time, we were praying that those pilots knew where we were being held and didn't throw any stray bombs our way. In May the harbor at Haiphong was mined; we didn't know it at the time, but we would have been delighted to hear that too.

In mid-May there was a large move. Two hundred nine of us were taken by truck caravan to a prison in the mountains, about one hundred fifty miles north of Hanoi and only about five miles south of the Chinese border. We named the place "Dogpatch." It was built onto the side of a mountain. There were a number of buildings, each with several smaller cells in it. Each building held about twenty men. There was no electricity; for light in the evening we had small kerosene lamps.

The V told us we were being held there for our own safety. Since the "warmongering, capitalist puppets of Wall Street were illegally bombing the women, children, and old folks in Hanoi, it would no longer be safe for us to be held there." We believed, however, that they wanted us close to the Chinese border so that should the U.S. invade, they could slip us across into China and perhaps use us as bargaining chips.

At Dogpatch, we were pretty much marking time. The V largely left us alone and didn't harass us. They gave some rooms chess or checker sets. They also had several books, notably a Russian language book, which they would move from building to building on a daily basis. We began to learn Russian.

I have not been blessed with the ability to sing; in fact, I generally can't carry a tune in a wheelbarrow. Nonetheless, one of the guys I lived with decided that he could teach me to sing. Each day, when the rest of our building was let out into the courtyard to empty the buckets and wash the dishes, Al and I would retreat to the far corner of the last cell in the building for our singing lessons. His patience was astounding. Every day I would sing, "Doe a deer, a female deer...," over and over. I don't think I ever got any better.

12

Free at Last, Thank God Almighty,
Free at Last

In January 1973, the United States, in the person of Henry Kissinger, negotiated the end of U.S. involvement in Vietnam. One of the conditions was that we were to be released, and furthermore, they had to tell us about it. A V officer came around to the buildings in Dogpatch with a tape recording of Hanoi Hannah on the Voice of Vietnam. It was a whole program on the victory of the People's Liberation Army of North Vietnam over the imperialist aggressors, the United States military in South Vietnam.

The United States had capitulated and would withdraw from South Vietnam. Buried in that half-hour of propaganda was a line about a prisoner exchange, or release, according to how long we had been POWs. It sounded good to us, but they had lied to us before — about the basketball pictures, for example. We were very skeptical.

Several days later trucks arrived, and we were loaded into them and taken to Hanoi. We were separated into four large groups and held at four different prisons, according to our longevity as POWs. The amount and quality of food increased. We were allowed outside all together. It really did look as if we were going to be released. Our spirits were rising higher each day. Promptly, out of spite, I began to grow my goatee again. The V were quite dismayed, but they dared not touch me as preparations were being made for our release. I would be the only POW to leave Vietnam with a goatee. We didn't win any big victories — only small ones.

In their efforts to make up groups of equal numbers, the Vietnamese regularly took one, two, or several Americans from one prison to another. Wayne Waddell, a fellow POW, was likely to be in the group that would be released ahead of mine. I wrote a long letter to Karen and gave it to Wayne to deliver if he were released ahead of me. He promised he would sneak it out and see that she got it, and he did. In the letter I explained to Karen and my family that on release, I wanted to go to the West Coast to be near Karen rather than to my home in Pennsylvania. I asked my family to come out west.

On March 14, 1973, I and my group were given civilian clothes and loaded onto buses. We were guardedly optimistic, but still not completely convinced it was not a trick.We were not blindfolded for the first time ever during a move, and we could see the devastation from the B52 raids that had been instrumental in bringing the conflict to an end. I think I finally believed we were going to be released when that bus pulled up to Gia Lam, the Hanoi airport, and there was a U.S. Air Force C141 sitting there on the ramp. At that point I no longer needed an airplane to fly!

The atmosphere was still a little reserved, as though everyone was holding his breath, thinking we might not make it. Step one: get off the bus. Breathe. Step two: walk through a line and have our names checked off a list by a V officer and U.S. Air Force officer. Breathe. Step three: walk up to a U.S. Air Force colonel, salute; he says something like "Welcome home." Breathe. Step four: be escorted out to the aircraft by a military officer or nurse, and climb into the airplane. Breathe.

Finally, the engines started. The C141 taxied out and began the take-off roll — we held our breath again. When the wheels left the ground, we all went crazy, cheering and shouting. We were free! Free at last, thank God almighty, free at last. It's impossible to describe the feeling: joy, tears, euphoria.

The flight went to Clark Air Force base in the Philippines, where we were put into the hospital for several days. We saw the docs and the shrinks and began the debriefing process. We were fitted for uniforms and given some civilian clothes. We hugged everyone we met. We ate ice cream and steak. We didn't want any special diet.

One of my buddies from flight training and A4s, Huey L'Herault, was with a carrier at Subic Bay, a Navy base in the Philippines about forty miles from Clark. He had been at Clark when we arrived and decided to come up to the hospital to see me. We weren't officially allowed to have visitors, but Huey was determined. A second obstacle in his way was that he was at Clark without a uniform.

The air intelligence officer who was assigned as my debriefer/escort told me that there was a friend of mine trying to see me. There was no way to get Huey onto the floor of the hospital, but my escort and I could go down the elevator to the dining room; then, instead of entering the dining room, we could go on down the hall, where Huey and I could meet for a few minutes.

Meanwhile, Huey had commandeered a uniform from some poor unsuspecting ensign. I am unable to describe the overwhelming emotion as I walked down that hallway, looking at Huey, a size forty guy in a size twenty-eight uniform. I knew I was free at last — thank God almighty, free at last. Tears of joy streamed down my face. I clung to him. Huey was the first reconnection with a life I had been away from for five and a half years.

Four days later, outfitted in new uniforms, partially debriefed and examined, we left for the United States. I was sitting in the cockpit, talking with the pilot and co-pilot, as we approached the coast of California, headed for Travis Air Force Base north of San Francisco. The pilot requested and was granted a low pass over the Golden Gate Bridge. It was the greatest sight I've ever seen in my life. It was a beautiful sunny day. As we descended and passed over the bridge, there wasn't a dry eye on the flight deck, either.

When I stepped out of the airplane at Travis, Karen and my mother, sister, and brother were there to meet me. Karen came running toward me and I caught her in my arms, lifting her and spinning around. (That picture appeared in the San Francisco *Chronicle.*) Within seconds, I was holding in my arms the people who were closest to me in all the world. Tears flowed like rain, and the joy was unbounded.

13

Walking on Air

Many of my fellow POWs came home to broken marriages. Wives had tired of waiting, tired of raising children without their fathers, tired of the years of uncertainty. But Karen, not even married, had waited for me, working in San Francisco. When I had left California for Vietnam in early June of 1967, we were either engaged or almost engaged, depending on whose story you listened to.

She was a genuine heroine in my eyes and those of my fellow POWs. Everyone knew the story: Karen waited! In prison we whiled away some time planning in elaborate detail the wedding Karen and I would have when we were all released. The most elaborate proposal was for a wedding in Hong Kong, complete with rickshaw caravan. Our eventual wedding was nothing like any of those plans, but it was a great way to pass the time, planning a gala party. The guys loved her, and so did I.

I was ready to get married immediately, but Karen thought we should wait just a little while. She may have wanted to see if I was going to go crazy. However, I managed to maintain an even keel, and we were married six weeks later, on May 5, 1973, in the chapel on the Naval Base at Treasure Island in San Francisco Bay. To this day I have no idea how that wedding was planned. Hundreds of friends and family were there, including about forty ex-POWs with whom I had lived over the years. We were all walking on air.

I had finished my debriefing, and Karen and I took six months of convalescent leave for honeymooning and goofing off. We made several trips back to Pennsylvania. The first was in early April before we were married. My little home town, Jeannette, turned out in full force. The city flew us in a helicopter from the Pittsburgh airport. Thousands of people were there, family and friends. It was so heart-warming, and tears flowed once again.

Our second trip to Jeannette followed our marriage and official honeymoon in Hawaii. We drove back to California, dragging along with us my best friend from high school, Dick Baker, and his wife, Cheryl. It was a wonderful trip, camping along the way and slowly working our way back to Karen's family home in California.

Then I began to grow antsy: I wanted to get back to flying. In October 1973, I asked for and received orders to flight refresher training in Kingsville, Texas. The day we arrived in Kingsville, as I was entering the squadron to check in, I bumped into Ray Alcorn, another ex-POW. He was dressed in flight gear and headed out to an aircraft. His rear cockpit was empty, so he invited me to come along.

I immediately went to the parachute loft and had them outfit me. Finding Ray on the flight line, I climbed into the rear cockpit. It was an exhilarating experience to be back in a cockpit after six years. Ray even let me fly it. Free at last.

After we landed, we were asked to report to the training wing commander's office. There are many rules in the service about qualifications to ride in — let alone fly — naval aircraft: a pressure chamber check-out every three years; swimming qualifications every five years; ejection seat familiarization every year — too many rules to enumerate here. None of which I had followed prior to going flying with Ray. The wing commander tactfully managed to get the message across that we had broken almost every rule he could think of. He was careful not to upset us, probably thinking we might go crazy, since we'd both been POWs! The next day a new rule was announced: "Ex-POWs are not to fly together in the same aircraft, and not to fly at all until all their training qualifications are current." I guess they thought that if we went crazy, there was no need to lose more than one person and one aircraft at a time!

Flying was easy to get back into. I think that at some point, as one learns to fly, one learns that the aircraft doesn't respond instantaneously. If you've flown enough to learn that, you can always go back quickly to flying.

The last phase of my flight refresher was to go through carrier landing qualifications. In January 1974, a group of us from flight refresher training were practicing carrier landings on a carrier off Norfolk, Virginia. One evening when we were in the bar having a beer, a loud voice yelled from the doorway, "Dave! Dave Carey, is that you?" It was Dean Cramer, who had flown over me when I was first shot down and standing out there in that rice paddy.

Dean and I met in the middle of the room, fell into each other's arms, and wept like babies. Eventually we settled down, ordered a beer, and sat down to talk. Dean was overwhelmed with how badly he felt having to leave me there in the rice paddy that day. He went on and on. I tried to tell him it was okay, but he just kept repeating himself.

Finally I said, "Dean, let's think about this. You're up there, sitting in an air-conditioned airplane, going back to the ship to have a milkshake. I'm down in that rice paddy, mud up to my calves. You don't know a lot about what bad feels like!" So Dean regained his composure, and we had a wonderful reunion.

Following flight refresher, I went back to flying A4s with Fighter Squadron 126 at Miramar Naval Air Station in San Diego, California. I stayed at Miramar, with various organizations, from 1974 through 1984. In that time I had command of two squadrons and spent two tours on the admiral's staff. We were blessed with two children — Jeff, born in 1974, and Alyssa, born in 1976. Life was great; we prospered wonderfully.

My last job in the Navy, from 1984 to 1986, was to run a leadership and management training program for prospective commanding and executive officers. I discovered that I had a talent for working with people in that context. I retired in 1986 and went into business for myself as a motivational speaker, consultant, and trainer, specializing in "how people work together" and providing business and personal coaching to individuals and teams.

Part 2

How Did You Do It?

Since 1986, when I retired from the Navy, I have been working as a motivational speaker, as a consultant and trainer focusing on how people can work together more effectively, and as a business and personal coach.

As a motivational speaker, 90 percent of the time I use my POW experience as an analogy for facing problems and changes, growing, and dealing with tragedy and the ups and downs of work and daily life.

As a consultant, trainer, and coach, I occasionally use or refer to my POW experience. I have been told over and over again that many lessons can be drawn from my experiences, and I know that is true. It is not necessary for all of us to learn everything first-hand; we can learn vicariously, through others. One primary purpose of any book is to teach us, or at least show us, in a matter of a few hours, what has taken someone else years and years to learn.

In the pages that follow, I will try to point out some of what I believe can be learned from my experiences. I know that I can make only a limited number of connections. I also know that you can make far more connections than I can make. That's why, in the introduction, I asked you to read with this question uppermost in your mind: "So what?"

When people hear that I spent five and a half years in prison in North Vietnam, they invariably ask, "How did you do it?" Over the years, in speaking to a great many audiences, I have tried to answer that question in a way that will be helpful and encouraging to them, wherever they are in living the story of their life.

Typically I set the scene by describing being shot down and some of the general conditions under which we were held. Then I ask the members of the audience what they would have done in that situation. How do they think we did it? I'm sure their answers, with minor variations, are the same as yours would be. The list generally looks like this:

Survive
Escape
Think positively
Support each other
Plan
Get organized
Keep a sense of humor
Help each other
Do it one day at a time
Remember home
Think about the future
Communicate
Accept the inevitability of the situation
Have faith
Cry
Pray
Work as a team
Trust each other
Believe in ourselves

How did we do it? That's exactly how we did it. I can't imagine that anyone would add anything inappropriate to the list. And every time I ask that question and get a list similar to the one above, I am struck by how much it looks like anyone's work, and the rest of life as well.

I know that there are days for all of us when we are just hoping to survive. Or days when we are thinking to ourselves, "If I could just escape from here for a little while!" Long-term escape looks like retirement to a lot of people. And most of us are getting paid to do the things on that list, to plan, to communicate, to help each other, to get organized, to work together effectively.

As my own brief framework for answering the question, "How did we do it?" I'd suggest the following simple factors for our success in that harsh environment:

1. We did what we had to do.
2. We did our best.
3. We chose to grow through that experience.
4. We kept our sense of humor.
5. We kept the faith:
   - faith in ourselves
   - faith in each other
   - faith in our country
   - faith in God

I believe these guidelines can be directly translated into every life, both professionally and personally. After all, how do you cope when things aren't going well? How do you persevere in the face of adversity? How do you manage when you have problems? How are you surviving in a competitive environment? How do you choose to do your job and live your life, just day to day? How will you get yourself into the future? How do you deal with change?

Do you do what you have to do? Do you do your best? Do you keep your sense of humor? Are you growing through everything? Do you keep the faith? All these are choices, and we all can and do make them every day, in every aspect of our lives.

We did what we had to do.

In Hanoi, the first thing we always did was to communicate. Our captors wanted us to be cut off, isolated in our cells, kept out of touch with one another. In your life and work, there is no plan to cut you off, to isolate you, to get you out of touch with the people with whom and for whom you work, or the people with whom you live.

However, if I asked you, "How easy is it for you to get out of touch, to lose contact with the people around you, to feel isolated or cut off?" you'd answer, "Easy. Very easy." It is extremely easy to lose our connection with other people, whether at work or at home among our family.

Why were we so concerned about our ability to communicate effectively in Hanoi? If we were going to do anything on a scale larger than a few people locked up in a single cell, we were going to have to have some sort of communications link. If we were to get organized, plan, escape, survive, support each other, work together effectively, or define ethical conduct and our mission, we had to be able to communicate effectively.

Why should communications issues be important to you where you are? I believe the answers are all the same. Well, maybe not the plan to escape — although I'm sure there are days at work when that looks pretty tempting.

The communications process in Hanoi's prisons was very difficult. I had a callus on my knuckle about three-eighths of an inch thick from tapping on the wall. Occasionally, if the guards wanted to harass us, they would come around and make us hold out our hands. Whoever had calluses on his knuckles would be beaten.

I thought that was preferable, on rare occasions, to lying on a filthy floor looking under the door for guards, or listening for footsteps on the floor for hours on end. When one of us was tapping on the wall, none of his roommates were goofing off. They had their eyes and ears pressed to the cracks, listening for footsteps. We were taking care of each other. It was a team effort, and it was hard work.

How difficult is the communications process in your life and work? I am certain that no one thinks he or she can accomplish something once and for all by making one simple statement. We all know better than that. Typically we have to say things over and over again, both at home and at work.

Perhaps we decide to write our point down in a memo. Weeks later, we remember it when we find a copy in our desk drawer. We inquire as to how our pearls of wisdom are being complied with, and of course everyone denies ever having seen our memo. Worse yet, now we use e-mail, voice mail, and intranets, so everyone is out there deleting our pearls of wisdom and blaming it on the system.

And moving away from the workplace, how hard is the communications process at home? Men and women sometimes communicate quite differently. Teenagers have a built-in out-of-touch mechanism. We assume we are communicating well and that everyone hears and understands; but good, clear communication requires very hard work.

However, if we are not able to communicate well and clearly, then every other effort is like spitting into the wind, particularly as one moves into supervision and management, or marriage and parenthood. If you aren't communicating effectively then everything you try to do will be extremely difficult, or even impossible. Of all the attributes and skills necessary for personal and business success, our ability to communicate is absolutely critical.

Where does the burden for clear, accurate communications lie? I believe it lies with the sender. If an archer shoots an arrow and it does not hit the target, it is not the fault of the target — it is the fault of the archer.

We did our best.

Although we weren't sure of it at the time, it turned out that doing our best was more than sufficient. In the late 1990s, it seems the emphasis in much of our society is to do just enough to get by. But life has some unwritten rules, and one of them is that we profit from any endeavor exactly in proportion to what we invest in it. The old adages are right: "If something is worth doing, it's worth doing right"; and "There's never enough time to do something right the first time, but there's always time to do it over." Doing our best in every endeavor, giving it our all, pouring our passion and energy into our efforts: that's a key to success in our lives.

There are a number of lessons we can draw from the episode of the Colonel and the Commander. First, I am astounded by how easily the other five men were led astray and influenced. Those five weren't any different than any of us: they had been through all the training and seen all the John Wayne movies; they knew how they were supposed to conduct themselves. Yet when placed in that position, they did precisely what they knew they should not. Granted they did so reluctantly and with lots of arguing, but they did it. People are easily influenced.

Furthermore, I believe we are all exerting far more influence than we may realize. I believe that the job of leadership — and almost everyone exercises some degree of leadership — is to influence people. Indeed, we all live and work at the center of a complex sphere of influence. Therefore, we need to stop and consider what kind of an influence we might be having. Are we setting an example we would point to with pride? Is our influence for good ends and just causes? It is especially important for us to consider what kinds of influence we are having, because people are so easily influenced!

Second, I think there is a lesson in this story about how people go astray when they find themselves in ethical and moral dilemmas. After the isolated men were moved in with us in the Pig Sty, we had numerous long discussions about how they had been so badly misled.

They knew something was wrong. They knew that what they were hearing wasn't what they believed or had been taught. They had serious doubts about the Colonel and the Commander and what the two of them were saying. But here were two senior officers — squadron commanding officers — and they really didn't feel they could directly oppose them. So they went along, and little by little, they went farther and farther astray.

That's precisely how ordinary people get themselves into ethical and moral dilemmas. We usually allow ourselves to be influenced by someone, or something, or our own rationalizations, and little by little we go astray. We don't set out to be unethical or immoral. We deviate a little at a time, until one day, when it all blows up in our faces, we wake up. Then our immediate reaction is, "How did I ever allow this to happen to me?"

There are numerous examples we should pay attention to. John Dean, of President Nixon's staff, said at the Watergate hearings: "We didn't mean to break the law. We just lost track of the direction our moral compass was pointing." We all need to be making frequent azimuth checks on our ethical and moral compasses.

Some of the work I do is with law enforcement agencies. In 1989, the Los Angeles Sheriff's Department had a group of narcotics officers who were arrested and prosecuted for stealing and using drug money. The investigation showed that they had progressed from taking a little money for some much-needed equipment to taking a lot of money and using it for personal purchases. Those people didn't start out to be dirty cops. They lost track of their ethical compasses, and little by little they went astray.

Perhaps even more thought-provoking are the other police officers who were transferred through that narcotics unit during that time period. How were they influenced? What did they do about what they learned? Or did they just not notice what was going on?

It is interesting to reflect on how we were able to take the other five back into the fold after they had behaved very badly. Recall the line in the plums: "It is neither American nor Christian to nag a repentant sinner to the grave." CAG Stockdale, years earlier, had sent that line to all of us down through many layers of clandestine communication.

We thought and talked about that. Whatever was CAG talking about? Did his elevator still go to the top floor? Then one day it dawned on us that every one of us was a repentant sinner. We had all, at some time, been taken out by our captors and had not been tough enough; we had given too much, too easily.

CAG Stockdale was telling us how we were to live with each other when those things happened, as inevitably they would. "It is neither American nor Christian to nag a repentant sinner to the grave." And so we had years of practice in taking each other back into the fold; years of confessing our shortcomings; years of being completely open and honest with each other; years of practice in the art of reunifying after what could have been very divisive infractions. When we finally got the word to those five and they immediately did an about-face, we already knew how we were to deal with them. We knew how to take repentant sinners back into the fold.

This is directly related to the way we deal now with people who make mistakes, fall short of the mark, take risks and fail. I want to qualify this, though, by saying I absolutely believe that in business there are people who should be fired. It has to be done right, with appropriate efforts to train and guide; with the necessary documentation and counseling. But still, there are people who should be fired; it isn't the people you fire who give you problems — it's the ones you don't fire.

Nevertheless, there are almost certainly other people in any organization who have made some mistake the stigma of which they cannot move beyond — because their co-workers won't let them. If they could get out from under it, they would probably be a much more valuable asset to the organization.

It is common to say, "People need to make mistakes or else they are not taking risks and learning. We want and expect people to take risks." But when they do, and fail, how do we react? In the poem "The Rime of the Ancient Mariner," a sailor kills an albatross and thus brings bad luck on his ship. His angry shipmates punish him by hanging the huge dead bird around his neck. When one of our employees makes an error, do we hang the albatross around his neck forever?

The fact is that we all make mistakes, do things when we know not to, go against our training and common sense. Fortunately, we usually manage to recover and get by.

Our way of dealing with repentant sinners is even more critical in our families. People will make mistakes — we all do. The important thing is how we deal with them. Everyone probably has or knows relatives who won't even talk with each other because of past mistakes; many times they can no longer even remember the details of the conflicts. What a shame!

In business and life, things aren't always fair. By all rights, the Colonel and the Commander ought to have been courts-martialed for their conduct in Hanoi. They weren't. The system wasn't fair.

There is never a guarantee that things will be fair. It is an assumption we make that is erroneous. There is no rule of the universe that says life, work, business, or any other "system" has to be fair. It is very nice when things are fair, but we should not expect it. The real question is how we move forward in the face of unfairness. I'm not talking here about being passive, about not trying to correct wrongs. We must stand up for what is right, argue for fairness and justice, and do our absolute best at all times.

At the same time, we must recognize that unfair things will happen: you might not get a promotion you deserve; someone might get away with dishonesty; you may not get credit for an accomplishment. It is a matter of choice whether you cling to an injustice, wrap your life around it, and let it become a predominant theme in your life — or whether you forgive, let it go, and move on with your life.

People often ask me, "How do you feel about your captors now?" I feel just fine about them. They were just people doing what they were ordered to do. There were a few sickos in the crowd, but you can't judge an entire population by those few. I have chosen to forgive and move forward with my life.

We chose to grow through the experience.

It is also a matter of choice to learn and to grow. The choice is complicated by the fact that along with growth comes change, and change can be quite difficult. It entails risk and fear of the unknown. A saying goes, "Most people would prefer a comfortable hell to an unknown heaven." On the other hand, Richard Nixon said, "When you're through changing, you're through." (Of course, he found a new way to be through.)

In any event, change is our constant companion, and its pace is accelerating exponentially. The intellectual growth curve for our lives is typically very steep for the first twenty-two years or so; then, for most people, it tapers off dramatically. After that we have to make a conscious effort to grow and change.

In those cells in Hanoi, we chose to grow in the midst of famine. We had no materials. It is so much easier now, with access to books, audiotapes, and other educational materials and opportunities. We have no excuse not to keep growing, but we confront innumerable distractions: television, laziness, the prevalent sense that society or our government owes us entitlements — the list is very long.

There is a little rhyme that goes:

> Life can't give me joy and peace,
> It's up to me to will it,
> Life just gives me time and space,
> It's up to me to fill it!

We must choose to grow throughout our lives.

We kept our sense of humor.

Laughter was the way we coped with the pressure, kept our sanity, and held everything together. It was the way we let off the pressure. One of the things I learned in prison was this: I know clearly, unequivocally, beyond a shadow of any doubt, who is responsible for the balance, coping, and perspective in your life. You are! Each of us must assume the responsibility for his or her own life.

It does not matter how hard it is to keep balance and perspective in our lives; it does not matter that we do not have time for it. How easy do you think it would be to worry yourself into an ulcer? Pretty easy, I think. How easy is it for us to ruin relationships that are important to us? Pretty easy, I think. How easy do you think it would be to drink yourself into a bottle? Pretty easy, I think! It is so easy for us to mess up our lives. If each one of us does not figure out how to cope with the pressure and stress, how to keep things in perspective and balance, it will not get done. Nobody else wants to, can, or will do it for us.

If I wanted to present my ideas in the context of work, that would put them in a certain perspective. If I wanted to write about them in the context of life in general, that would put them in another perspective. And if I wanted to view them in the context of all of eternity, that would put them in yet another perspective.

One of our primary tasks in life — perhaps the biggest — is to keep everything in perspective and balance. We must do what we have to do, do our best to work hard, strive, and stretch ourselves, but we ought not to work ourselves into a heart attack or worry ourselves into an ulcer. If you are lying in the hospital trying to keep the little blip going on the screen, you won't be much use to your family, community, company, or anyone else.

Our emotional reservoir is similar to a swimming pool. If the pool is full, it can lose quite a lot of water without any serious consequences, but when it is nearly empty, any loss is significant. Typically, we don't pay attention to the state of our reservoir until it is nearly exhausted, and then it may be too late.

The question of balance and perspective is always a question of give and take. There is more to life than work — or play. We really need to balance in a simple sense the physical, mental, and spiritual parts of our being. In a little more detailed sense, we are striving to achieve balance among the family, financial, social, spiritual, mental, career, health/physical, and character aspects of our lives.

If any of these gets really out of balance, all the other aspects suffer.

Last, we don't have to do it alone. I have also learned that the Lord God, Creator of the Universe, wants to have a personal relationship with me. He cares about me: about the balance and coping in my life, about every detail of my life. Even the hairs of my head are numbered. I do not have to do it alone. He is always there. I don't understand it — I don't think I ever will — but I know beyond a shadow of a doubt that Jesus Christ, the risen Savior, cares about me, and about you. He is intensely interested in the balance and coping in my life, and He wants to, and is able to help.

We kept the faith.

Faith in ourselves, in our ability to endure, to gut it out, to do our best. The sun was going to come up each day, and I was going to be there to see it.

There are prisonlike aspects of my life right now, and I'll bet that there are prisonlike aspects of your life too. There are things I would just as soon not have to do, but I have responsibilities and duties. Faith in ourselves entails believing in our ability to fulfill duties, responsibilities, and obligations, no matter how difficult.

It is also faith in our ability to have an impact, to count for something, to have influence. We have to stand up and espouse what we believe in, and not be embarrassed about saying "This is right, this is wrong, and this is where I stand."

We are not completely controlled by our environment, nor are we completely controlled by our genetic inheritance. Faith in ourselves enables us to live our lives without crutches, without drugs, and without alcohol. We must assume responsibility for ourselves and our lives. No one and nothing else can, will, or should.

In Hanoi, I learned this about you and me: Life can't get too tough for us. In us, the Lord has made incredibly resourceful, tough, creative, resilient creatures. The apostle Paul assures us, "I can do all things through Christ who strengthens me," (Philippians 13:4). He doesn't say "some things" or "maybe"; no, he says "I can do all things."

Faith in ourselves means believing we can make a difference. These lines are a true and good reminder:

What can I do? I am only one person, I can't do every-
     thing.
But I am one person, and I can do something.

If not me, who?
If not now, when?

I see that kind of faith in ourselves as directly trans-latable into life. After all, how will you get yourself into the future? How will you deal with all the changes that are coming? How will you face problems? How will you deal with the tragedy that is coming in your life? Faith in ourselves: we can do our best, we can do what we have to do, no matter what. Faith in ourselves.

Faith in each other. We survived through a commit-ment to support and protect each other, to assume that everyone was doing his best. I have lived with men who in a sense held my life in their hands. I always knew that they would do the best they could. When the situation was reversed, they in turn granted that to me.

It is that kind of faith and trust in each other that really is the bedrock foundation that allows us to work together and live together effectively. It is the basis of effective teamwork, effective marriage, effective families, and effective business.

There are examples everywhere. In sports, trust is relatively easy to see. The quarterback drops back and throws a pass down the field to where no one stands, knowing that when the ball gets there, the tight end will be there. That is teamwork, built on faith and trust in each other.

It is such hard work! Do you know how many times those athletes practice running down the field, timing themselves, throwing the ball to a precise place at a precise time? That kind of faith and confidence in each other is based on time spent together working on the same issues, whether in football, marriage, or business. Where you live and work, are you trusting enough to throw the ball?

I do a lot of team-building and organizational development work all over the United States, in many different organizations. In my experience, trust is an issue in more than nine out of ten situations: trust between individuals, among work groups and teams, within organizations.

Trust is such a difficult issue to deal with. Over and over again, people tell me, "He or she has to earn my trust." Well, that's true. However, in order for someone to earn trust, others must be willing to grant him the opportunity. How does one earn your trust if you will not give them the opportunity? It is a vicious cycle.

Our initial assumption in Hanoi was that each person was doing the best he could in the situation in which he found himself. He had to make a decision and do something with what he knew at the time. That was our starting point. From there we could discuss, critique, argue, add to, change, subtract from — however, that assumption was always our starting point.

Actually, trust is something that all of us control in our heads. It makes all the difference in the world what your initial assumption is. You can assume that people are trying to do their best, or you can assume that people aren't trying to do their best, are only looking out for themselves, or don't really care. Your frame of reference makes a huge difference in your own level of trust and in the feeling of trust which you convey to others.

I have worked with hundreds of groups. I have yet to find anyone who does not want to do a good job. I have yet to find anyone who purposely undermines their business responsibilities. I don't believe it is reasonable to assume that people do not want to try to do a good job. In the North Vietnamese prisons, we did not do our jobs perfectly, but we always tried to assume that the other person would do the best he could.

Faith in our country. The United States is one of the greatest nations that has ever existed. This is a land of freedom, achievement, and opportunity. That isn't true in many other places.

The problem is, we are inundated by information about what is wrong with this country, and that is all out of perspective. On the six o'clock news any evening, how much of what we hear and see deals with what's wrong with our country? And how much will be about what is right? It's all out of proportion.

Several years ago, I was lying on the couch and Karen was sitting nearby reading the newspaper. She asked, "Do you want to read some of the newspaper?" I replied, "No, just find something good in there and read it to me."

She searched through that paper for an hour without finding anything good to read to me. On that day in history, in this country, how much good do you suppose happened, as opposed to how much bad? Our information system is out of balance, and we have to take the initiative in keeping it in perspective.

Faith in God. Even when I was by myself, I was never alone in those prisons. I have also lived with men who professed to be atheists and agnostics. I believe it was more difficult for them. I do not think that was any accident.

Sometimes I think we have become too materially oriented, too egocentric. We take so much for granted. The fact is, you and I are blessed; we have so much, and we enjoy so much. We don't deserve it — we are simply blessed. More and more I think we forget the spiritual roots upon which this country was founded.

On Sundays in those prison cells we were pretty faithful in conducting worship services. The letter "C," for "church," was tapped from cell to cell as the signal for the service to begin. Worship always consisted of the Lord's Prayer, the Twenty-third Psalm, and the Pledge of Allegiance. A little mixing of church and state; however, we thought it permissible under the circumstances!

How did we do it? Those are the ways we did it. We did what we had to do. We did our best. We chose to grow through that experience. We kept our sense of humor. We kept the faith. What else can be learned from my experience? Let me suggest a few things in the following chapter.

A Few Insights

Nothing Is Easy

Scott Peck wrote in the first line of *A Road Less Traveled,* "Life is difficult." We will inevitably face problems in our lives and in our work. There will be joy and sorrow, happy times and sad times.

But many of us have a mindset that says, "No, no, life and work are supposed to be easy. Success will come to me on a silver platter; life will be a bed of roses." When things are going badly, we run around saying, "Why me? Why is this happening to me?"

When things are going well, however, we don't hear anybody saying, "Why me? Why is this happening to me?" It is a kind of mindset. And if that is my mindset, work and life are going to be very frustrating experiences.

Someday in the future, today — as complex and challenging as it is — will be part of the "good old days." Competition isn't going to leave the marketplace; it's going to increase. The global marketplace will continue to shrink. Business will continue to grow more demanding. We are definitely going to have our ups and downs.

There is enormous concern, and rightly so, over the teen suicide rate in the United States. Choosing suicide is incomprehensible to me. I fear that as a society, in a multitude of ways, we are giving our children the false impression that life is easy. In this television-fed culture it can be very easy to start thinking that there is no problem that cannot be solved in under an hour — or at most in a miniseries. So when teenagers come up against harsh reality, they are overwhelmed.

Robert Service wrote, "It's the keepin on livin' that's hard." The Bible tells us, "In this world you will have trouble" (John 16:33). Scott Peck writes, "It is in this whole process of meeting and solving problems that life has meaning. Problems are the cutting edge that distinguishes between success and failure. Problems call forth our courage and wisdom; indeed, they create our courage and our wisdom" *(The Road Less Traveled,* p. 16).

Life and work are not always going to be easy. There will be difficult times. "Easy" is not a good word for us to have in our vocabulary. My biggest complaint about almost all popular self-help, self-improvement, leadership, and management literature and training is that it gives people the idea that everything is easy if you just want it enough and have the right attitude. In reality, few accomplishments will be easy. Almost everything takes longer than we originally anticipated and is more difficult than we thought it would be at first.

For example, the advice given by Ken Blanchard and Spencer Johnson in *The One Minute Manager* is psychologically sound. It is written in a way anyone can understand. The problem is, it doesn't warn us how hard it will be to follow that advice when we are under extreme pressure. How easily will you be able to "first be tough on the behavior and then supportive of the person" when you are contending with errors made in the crisis of a rapidly approaching deadline?

The plan seems so easy when we read it, but now, under the pressure of the moment, we have great difficulty executing all that sound advice. Then, as a result, we feel less competent. Life isn't always easy; sometimes it will be very difficult.

Another example is a typical "delegation workshop" that is a part of dozens of training programs. Delegation seems simple: you go back to the office and dump your in-basket all over everyone else's desks. Well, actually, you go back to the office and delegate appropriately. Your people mutter to themselves, "She must have been to the delegation workshop." Then they start laying bets on how long your newfound skill will last.

At the delegation workshop, they neglected to tell you how hard it will be when the pressure is on and senior management is demanding an update — now. They didn't mention the real-world pitfalls and land mines. So, eventually, much of the delegated work migrates back onto your desk. Then you feel terrible, because you're struggling so hard with what seemed so easy at the workshop.

If your desire is to achieve something significant, you will have to be very committed. You'll have to plan and work hard. There will be setbacks; things rarely go exactly as anticipated. Not much is easy.

Mastery, Step by Step

The second thing I would suggest can be learned from my experience is that we get though difficulties, deal with adversity, solve problems, change, grow, go into the future, live our lives and do our jobs just a little bit at a time. Just a step at a time, a day at a time.

As much as you and I would love instant gratification, it is not given to us to know the future. What is given to us is to do what we must, to do our best, to continue to grow, to keep our sense of humor, and to keep the faith day in and day out, day in and day out, day in and day out.

When I was upside down in that airplane, coming through the sky like a ton of lead, if anybody had said to me, "Jump out of this airplane and you will be in prison for five and a half years," I don't know what I would have done. At that point I couldn't have conceived of surviving such an ordeal; and then I did it, one day at a time.

But it wasn't given to me to know how long I'd be there. What was given to me was to work at it just a little bit at a time, and to do my best, do what I had to do, grow through it all and keep my sense of humor, and keep the faith.

I read a marvelous article, "Playing for Keeps," by George Leonard, in the May 1987 issue of *Esquire* magazine. It discusses the way to mastery in our lives. We don't master anything in one giant stride forward after another. Instead, mastery is found by diligently spending the great majority of our time practicing, preparing, and planning, and this occasionally yields a giant stride or growth spurt. So we are to be persistent and diligent, to continue putting one foot in front of the other, day by day moving forward in our lives.

However, not everyone approaches life that way. Some people choose to dabble at life. They grow tired and discouraged with practicing, preparing, and working so hard for such infrequent growth spurts. Eventually, they give up on their endeavor and move on to something else and dabble at it. The pattern repeats, and they never achieve mastery in anything.

Others become obsessed with progress. They devote inordinate amounts of time and energy to their current undertaking until they burn themselves out. Then, after a recovery period, they gather themselves together again and move on to become obsessed with something else. Again, the pattern repeats, and they never achieve mastery. Unfortunately, they may also take others down with them — for example, if they start a business and completely burn themselves and others out.

Finally, some people grow tired and discouraged through working so hard, practicing and preparing. They settle for much less than is possible. They become hacks and drones. They quit working at improvement and settle for the status quo, with nothing but retirement to anticipate.

If you want to achieve mastery in your life, you will have to work at it patiently and persistently. A step at a time, little by little. Doing your best, doing what you have to do, constantly growing, keeping your sense of humor, and keeping the faith.

We Have What We Need

From my experience, I also believe that, through the grace of God, we are all equipped with what it takes to be successful in our work and in our lives. It comes from the factory as built-in equipment. I am not very much different than anyone reading this book. We all have what it takes inside us.

I don't think that is any accident. I will never understand it. It is astonishing to me that the Almighty God cares about us. He wants to have a personal relationship with us. It is a gift: we cannot earn it; we don't deserve it; we simply need to humble ourselves before the Lord God and accept the gift of grace through Jesus Christ. He will not burden us with more than we can bear. He has equipped us so that we can succeed.

I think I can prove that you have what it takes. Reflect for a moment on the last terrible thing that happened to you — the last catastrophic, tragic event in your life. For me,

one of those events happened some years ago, when my son
Jeff, then twelve, broke his leg skiing.

His mother and I were up on the mountain, and they
brought him down in a rescue sled. He was wrapped up in a
blanket and shaking like a leaf. His mother and I went out
where he was lying, shivering, blood everywhere. He had
cut his chin and broken the bottom end of his femur, right
across the growth plate. (He forgot the lesson about "go
around the trees.")

Karen and I looked down at him, thinking "Oh my
God! What are we going to do? What's going to happen?
We are a million miles from nowhere — what are we going
to do here? How are we going to get through this? What's
going to happen to him?" It was definitely an "Oh-my-
Godder."

A moment ago, I asked you to think of the last catastrophic thing that happened in your life. I am willing to bet,
when it started, it too was an Oh-my-Godder. "Oh my God,
what am I going to do? How are we going to handle this?"
That's the way that big problems look when they start: they
are all Oh-my-Godders.

In retrospect, we all did pretty well. I was very proud
of my son. He showed us some qualities that we were
beginning to wonder if he possessed. He had the strength
and character to bear up under extreme pain and adversity.
He maintained a sense of humor through it all. He handled
it superbly.

It wasn't easy, believe me. They put him in a cast that
went from his toes to his chest. We had a twelve-year-old
board at home. But we all got through it pretty well, and in
essence we did what we had to do: we did our best, we grew
through that experience, we kept our sense of humor, and
we kept the faith.

Reflect on your own catastrophic problem. I'll bet that
you got through it. You managed. I'm sure it wasn't easy,

but you worked your way through it somehow. The ability to be successful in handling adversity is built in; it does come from the factory. Ordinary human beings deal with adversity, grow, move into the future, handle change, and achieve their goals. It takes effort, hard work, and time. We do it just a step at a time, but we can do it.

As a young man, I used to read books about people going through great adversity — concentration camp memoirs, for example. As I read, I would wonder how they could survive. Well, now I know. God has equipped us so that we are remarkably resilient, tough, strong creatures. Could you do what I did? I think so. I am sure of it.

Faith beyond Understanding

In fact, I know that if the circumstances are right — or wrong, I should say — you too will rise to the occasion. You will do what you have to do, do your best, grow through trials and tribulations, keep your sense of humor, and keep the faith: faith in yourself, in those around you, in your country, and, most important, in God.

The most important is faith in God? Yes. I am often asked what played the key role in my survival. My response always is, "It was my faith." My experience as a POW is reflected in the image of a trail of footprints in the sand. First there are two sets, side by side; then one set for a space; then two again. The text is, "Lord, I've been reviewing the footprints of my life, and I can see those times when we walked together. However, I see there were times when there is one set of footprints. Where were you then?" And the Lord replies, "My child, those were the times when I was carrying you."

That was my experience in the prisons of Vietnam. There were times when I was just along for the ride. It was out of my control; I was, as we say in aviation, out of airspeed, altitude, and ideas, all at the same time! At those times, Jesus Christ carried me.

I've also been asked if it's true that "there are no atheists in foxholes." If there are, I believe it is only because the foxhole isn't deep enough and dirty enough yet. There are no atheists when it gets bad enough. A person in an automobile accident, or falling from a cliff, instinctively calls out for help — to God. Deep down, we know and believe. God has created us with a vacuum in our souls that only He can fill.

A Matter of Choice

I'm sure you already knew, intuitively, all the points I've tried to make here. The real question is this: What do you choose to do about them? How do you choose to live your life and do your job? In fact, I think that is probably the most important thing that can be learned from my experience. We have the ability to choose.

How do you choose to live your life? How do you choose to do your job day in and day out? How do you choose to deal with adversity? How do you choose to take yourself into the future? How do you choose to handle change? How do you choose to grow and learn? How do you choose to keep the faith?

I am reminded of this verse by Henry Beechard:

> God asks no one if they will accept life.
> That is not the choice.
> You must take it.
> The only choice is how.

The most important question to ask is not "How do you do it?" but "How do you choose to do it?" It is not what inevitably happens to you in life that is important; it is how you choose to deal with what happens. All my experience teaches me that everything is a matter of choice, and we are all capable of making those choices.

In the first line of *A Tale of Two Cities,* Charles Dickens wrote, "'Twas the best of all times, and 'twas the worst of all times." He was absolutely right! Whatever challenges you are facing, this the best of all times for you to be who you are, working where you are working, living where you are living, doing what you're doing, working with the people with whom you work. It is also the worst of all times for you to be who you are, working where you are working, living where you are living — but you must choose to make it the best, and not the worst. My advice, hope, and prayer for you is that you choose to make this the best of all times. May God bless you.

Epilogue

After I retired from the Navy in 1986, my life continued to be wonderful. Our marriage grew stronger and stronger, and my business was flourishing. Then, in August of 1992, Karen discovered a small lump on the side of her right breast. We were upset, but she had had a benign cyst removed in 1967, so we didn't panic. But we soon learned that our worst fear was true. Karen had breast cancer. The news hit us like a truck. The unknown is terrifying, and this was totally unknown territory.

Cancer is an overwhelming, terrifying disease. My wife had cancer — and I was helpless. It took us a while to gather our senses about us and begin to plot a course of action.

We began to read everything we could find, and there is a great deal of information, from many points of view. We agonized over which course of action to take. There are sincere, believable, knowledgeable people advocating everything from standard chemotherapy, surgery, and radiation, to diet, nutritional supplements, herbs, and exotic treatments.

Karen decided she would pursue the most aggressive treatment she could find. She entered a national breast cancer study that was being conducted to evaluate the merits of pre-operative versus post-operative chemotherapy. Karen was placed in the pre-operative arm of the study. The chemotherapy was very difficult — not devastating, but very difficult — until her hair started coming out; then it was devastating.

Our twenty-four-mile drives from home to the Balboa Naval Hospital for her treatments were the longest trips of our lives. They were torture every mile of the way. Karen would start to get nauseated on the drive down, although she never got really sick through all of her initial treatments.

The chemotherapy was so effective that following the treatments the doctors could no longer find any trace of a lump. She then underwent a lumpectomy in January 1993, followed by radiation treatment to that breast. Her hair grew back, and by the summer of 1993 she had a clean bill of health and began quarterly follow-up visits to the hospital for monitoring. We began putting our lives back together.

In the spring of 1994, a routine x-ray showed a shadow on her left lung. Once again, a biopsy confirmed our worse fears: the cancer was back. We renewed our search for information, and she consulted several doctors. We got second opinions and third opinions. High-dose chemotherapy, followed by an autologous stem cell transplant (the successor to bone marrow transplant), was clearly the most aggressive option. Karen chose it.

Chemotherapy is poison that targets fast-growing cells. That is why it is effective against cancer cells. That is also why it makes hair fall out. High-dose chemotherapy is a process in which they damn near kill you with the strength of the dosage and then use stem cells taken from your blood prior to the chemotherapy to kick-start your body again. It is a devastating procedure. Fortunately, so much sedation was used during the five days of high-dose chemotherapy that Karen was oblivious to what was going on. She didn't even remember walking around the hospital ward with our daughter, Alyssa, and me.

The treatment was relatively successful. Her tumor shrunk by about 60 percent. Following her recovery from the chemotherapy and stem-cell transplant, Karen elected to have lung surgery in January 1995 to remove the residual tumor tissue. She recovered from the surgery and followed that with additional radiation to her upper left lung area. Her hair grew back once again, and in spring of 1995 she once again had a clean bill of health.

Our research continued, and over the summer of 1995 we decided to become vegetarians. Karen was an excellent cook and superb hostess who loved to entertain, so becoming a vegetarian was a big step for her. We also began a number of other alternative approaches to fighting cancer, taking enormous amounts of nutritional supplements and all manner of natural foods and drinks that we read were effective in some instances.

Karen's strength came back and she was doing wonderfully well. Then, in February 1996, she coughed up a little blood. We immediately had another x-ray, as well as a CAT scan and a bone scan. The CAT scan showed a tumor in her liver. She was — we were — back to the battle.

Nothing worked, and through the spring of 1996 Karen slowly deteriorated. Both Jeff and Alyssa came home from college for the summer. Throughout the struggle with cancer Karen's family had made numerous trips to support her, and they returned that summer. Throughout the summer, Karen grew weaker and weaker. Eventually she was unable to walk.

As the fall semester approached for Jeff and Alyssa, we agonized over what to do. Since there was no predictability, the four of us together decided that both of them would return to school that fall. Toward the end of August, after Jeff and Alyssa returned to school, Karen quickly became acutely ill. It was as if she had been strong until the kids left.

Her hospice nurse told her she didn't need to suffer so terribly, but the side effects of the medication would keep her asleep most of the time. Without hesitation, she asked for the medicine. We gave her enough to put her pretty much out of it. Then we began to back the dosage off, trying to find a level that would keep her from suffering very much and at the same time allow her to be as alert as possible. However, even as I decreased the dosage, Karen slipped deeper and deeper into a coma-like state.

On the second of September, Karen's mother had been sitting on the bed next to her for most of the morning. Karen was in a deep coma. Around noon I took her mother's place. I had my Bible and was reading to Karen several of the scripture verses to which we had been clinging. At about three o'clock in the afternoon, Karen quietly went to be with her Savior. Karen, the love of my life, my wife of twenty-three years, died after a four-year battle against breast cancer.

How did Karen do it?

It had been an incredibly difficult four years. Karen did her best, and did what she had to do. She was amazing in her ability to deal with her illness and her mortality. Oh, she and the rest of us cried a lot; our emotions went up and down like a roller-coaster, and our spirits did too. It is impossible to describe the emotional highs and lows we went through. I am certain that neither one of us could have predicted that she would be able to do as well as she did.

Several times she tried writing a journal, but she was never able to keep at it with regularity. As a result, I have a bundle of pages from various books and tablets, with thoughts and notes from her. Even though they are snippets of this and that, they are treasures for me, and I know they will be for our children in the future.

Karen planned her own memorial service. She chose a poem that she loved to be used on a handout at her service. Her desire was that people be able to come to some closure, and even to leave her service feeling good. She chose the music and talked with the singers. Together, she, I, our pastor Woody Garvin, several friends, and family members planned the program.

All that was an incredible gift to me and to her family. No matter how well you think you might be prepared for the death of someone that close to you, when it happens you aren't ready for it. I was so distraught when it actually happened, it was very difficult to think straight. Had it not been for her planning, I'm not sure how her service would have been organized. Everyone who knew her was able to see her hand in that service. Somehow, people left feeling good, and with a sense of really having said goodbye to Karen.

At one point, I told Karen that she really did need to write some practical things down for me — I didn't even know how to get to the cleaners. So she began to write information and instructions down for me in a green spiral-bound notebook. One of the notes was how to get to the dry cleaners.

Several hours after Karen died and we had all privately said our final farewells to her. I, her mother and father, and two of her very close friends were standing in the kitchen. We decided it was time to make some calls. But who should we call? Who would call whom? We were going around in circles, trying to get organized, and someone finally said, "Do you suppose Karen wrote anything about calling people in the spiral notebook?"

We quickly got out the notebook and began looking through it. There we found that she had pretty much written it all out for us: several calling chains, who to call personally — it was all there. Karen did her best; she did what she had to do.

Several days before she died, one of her closest friends went in to sit with her. Karen had been sleeping a lot, and Claudia lay down on the bed beside her. Karen opened her eyes. "Hello," Claudia said, "do you know who I am?"

"Yes," Karen replied, "do you know who I am?" She never lost her sense of humor.

She kept the faith: faith in herself, in her ability to cope, to find a way. Karen always rose to the occasion. She had never been very confident in her strength, but she proved to be incredibly tough. She went through one of the most punishing treatment regimes modern medicine offers. It brought her to her knees, but she rose above it; she prevailed.

I don't want to give you a false impression. She was no rock of Gibraltar. Her faith in herself waxed and waned. Through it all, though, she kept putting one foot in front of the other, trusting in God. She was an inspiration to everyone who encountered her.

She did it through faith in those around her. One of the most amazing aspects of Karen's illness was the number of people who were concerned about her and expressed that concern. Acquaintances, friends, and family rallied around. They were all wonderful. I don't know how we would have done it without them.

Karen had always been very social. Our home was the place where parties, Easter egg hunts, Thanksgiving, and many, many dinners were held. She had a wonderful ability to put people at ease, to make them feel valued and comfortable. When she went to work at our church's thrift shop in 1993, she soon became friends with all the volunteers and many of the customers. People were very comfortable around her; she fussed over them in a genuine way. She loved people, and in return people loved her.

As she fought her illness, other people gave her enormous support. She received cards and notes almost every day for years. There was a palpable outpouring of love; on several occasions Karen told me that she could literally feel people praying for her. I cannot explain adequately how much comfort we derived from that support.

We often wondered, "How do people go through this without friends, without faith, without church and community?" We couldn't imagine how much more difficult that must be.

For Karen, and me, her illness was a journey of growing faith. Never one for memorization (except for the price and sale price of just about anything you could name), Karen now began to memorize scripture. These Bible verses were especially comforting to her:

> If you confess with your mouth, Jesus is Lord, and believe in your heart that God raised him from the dead, you will be saved. For it is with your heart that you believe and are justified, and it is with your mouth that you confess and are saved.
>
> Romans 10: 9–10

> No eye has seen, no ear has heard, no mind has conceived what God has prepared for those who love Him.
>
> 1 Corinthians 2:9

Our pastor, Woody Garvin, was a wonderful support.
He told Karen one day shortly before she died that she was
unique in his experience of twenty-five years in the
ministry. He had observed that people who were dying
approached the closing of their lives with some level of
faith, and as the cold reality of death became more and more
apparent, their faith remained at that same level. They died
with the same level of faith they had when they entered that
closing chapter. He told her that in all his years as a pastor,
Karen was the only one he knew whose faith continued
steadily to increase as her death grew imminent. She kept
the faith and grew through it all.

During the first couple of years of her battle with
cancer, we wrestled with the questions "Why? Why her?
Why us? How could this be happening?" Finally, one day
it dawned on us that no matter what the answer might be,
it would not be acceptable. We wouldn't be satisfied with
any answer.

We quit asking why and accepted that this was part of
God's plan. We didn't understand it; we didn't agree with it.
She made the leap of faith and entrusted herself to the Lord.
Scripture tells us that God has a plan for us:

> For I know the plans I have for you, declares the
> Lord, plans to prosper you and not to harm you, plans
> to give you hope and a future. Then you will call upon
> me and come and pray to me, and I will listen to you.
> You will seek me and find me when you seek me with
> all your heart.
>
> Jeremiah 29:11-13

> Many are the plans in a man's heart, but it is the
> Lord's purpose that prevails.
>
> Proverbs 19:21

"For my thoughts are not your thoughts, neither are your ways my ways," declares the Lord.

Isaiah 55:8

How does one deal with tragedy such as Karen's illness and death? Rather ask, how does one choose to deal with such a tragedy? You do what you have to do, do your best, grow through it all, keep your sense of humor, and keep the faith. This experience with Karen brought these same lessons home to me once again.

Much that happens to us in life will be beyond our control. It isn't what happens to you that is important: it is how you choose to deal with it that counts.

This is the best of all times. If you're trying to live in the future — thinking, "When I retire, I'll ...; when my children get out of school, I'll ...; when ... then ..." — you're letting life pass you by. No matter what, this is the best of all times: today, this week, this year. We must choose to make it the best of all times, the best of all times.

May God bless you as you make your choices.

About the Author

Dave Carey is a graduate of the U.S. Naval Academy. He became a carrier-based pilot during the Vietnam war. After his plane was shot down, he was interned as a prisoner of war in Hanoi for five and a half years. His military honors include the Legion of Merit, five Bronze Stars, two Meritorious Service Medals, the Purple Heart, eight Air Medals, and the Navy Commendation Medal. After returning from Vietnam, he held three positions as commanding officer, including service as Director of the Navy's Leadership and Management Training program. He retired with the rank of Captain. He has two children and lives in San Diego, California.

The author is an acclaimed motivational speaker. As a consultant and trainer, Dave Carey focuses on assisting people in working together more effectively. He specializes in team building, leadership development, and organizational effectiveness. He also works with clients as a business and personal coach.

For information on presentations and training, please contact:

Dave Carey
P.O. Box 28085
San Diego, California 92198

voice: 858-485-1530
fax: 858-485-1007
dave@davecarey.com
www.davecarey.com

To order additional copies of

The Ways We Choose

Book: $15.95   Shipping/Handling: $3.50

Contact: ***BookPartners, Inc.***
P.O. Box 922
Wilsonville, OR 97070

E-mail: bpbooks@teleport.com
Fax: 503-682-8684
Phone: 503-682-9821
Order: 1-800-895-7323

Visit our Web site at:
www.bookpartners.com